PERPETUAL
MOTIVATION

PERPETUAL MOTIVATION

HOW TO
Light Your Fire and
Keep It Burning in
Your Career and in Life

Dave Durand

A Crossroad Book
The Crossroad Publishing Company
New York

The Crossroad Publishing Company
16 Penn Plaza, 481 Eighth Avenue
New York, NY 10001

Printed in the United States of America

Interior text design by Sans Serif

Library of Congress data is available
ISBN: 0-8245-2386-5

1 2 3 4 5 6 7 8 9 10   11 10 09 08 07 06

Contents

Acknowledgments   ix

Preface   xi

Introduction   1

PART ONE: EGO AND BALANCE

1 Runaway Self-Esteem   11

2 Avoiding the Trap of Self-Justification   41

3 The Pursuit of Life's Perfect Balance   49

4 Motivation, Balance, and Time Management   103

PART TWO: TACTICAL COMPONENTS

5 Integrity-Based Influence   115

6 Creativity and Humor   143

7 Conclusion   157

More Inspiring Products   174

Acknowledgments

This book was made possible by the support and efforts of many friends and acquaintances over the years. The study of what really motivates people can't be effective without the cooperation of literally thousands of individuals.

I thank all the wonderful people I've had the opportunity to work with over the past fifteen years while compiling this treatise. Nearly everyone I've interacted with in some small way helped shape the Formula for Motivation discussed in these pages.

In order to effectively determine what really motivates a person, one must spend a vast amount of time both in triumph and in tribulation with many different people. To those willing to share their experiences, I am deeply grateful.

I thank my wife, Lisa, for her incredible support of this project. One secret not revealed in this book is how to marry someone as wonderful as she is. I believe God gave us to each other, and I thank him for her role in my life, which, because of her, is filled with motivation.

I also thank—

My children—Kevin, Nicole, Ethan, Hannah, Mike, and

John Paul. You are filled with love and remind me daily of the importance and the rewards of balance in life.

My parents, Tom and Marty, for their living example and wonderful upbringing.

My siblings, Pete, Dan, Kathy, and Mary, for their unique roles in shaping my thoughts.

Erick Laine, Jim Stitt, Bruce Goodman, Al Dileonardo, Mike Lancelot and all the executives at Vector.

The entire ProBalance staff who assist me in my adventures.

Don Freda, whose example as a leader helped shape me in the first years of my business career.

Marty Domitrovich, who helped teach me the art of focus.

Warren Jamison and John Jones for their professionalism and editorial assistance.

Totus tous!

Preface

A bigger salary
A smaller waistline
More respect from your colleagues
A stronger retirement plan
A better relationship with your spouse

Everyone wants to achieve something, and anything you want to achieve requires motivation. But here's the challenge. If you're already motivated, you might think you don't have any more motivation to gain. If you aren't motivated, you might think that there's no way to start—you feel like you can't motivate yourself to be motivated!

Depending on your outlook, the title and message of this book, *Perpetual Motivation*, will seem like a blessing or a burden. If you already feel like you just can't get started on the big goals in your life, and if you are already exhausted by work, the last thing you want to think about is having to be motivated all the time. In fact, if you equate motivation with frantic energy, maybe you're secretly wishing you could find a way not to be motivated at all! In this book, Dave Durand will give you a different way of looking at things. The fact is, you already are motivated to do a lot of things. But instead of thinking of achievement as something you do during work hours, or only when you're at the gym, etc., Dave will show you that, as the lives of great achievers show, motivation actually grows out of a way of living that informs every part of our lives. Motivation is not about giving ourselves a desperate pep talk every morning before going off to sell a product, give a speech, run an office, or work with small children. It's about recognizing what matters most to us, and arranging our priorities so that every part of our lives reflects our priorities. The phrase *Perpetual Motivation* might seem like Dave is giving you even more work to do, but once you've applied the principles of this book for your life, you'll find that your life is more focused, more integrated, more energizing and fulfilling. Read Dave's book, watch the free DVD, then start applying these ideas in your everyday work and play. I think that, like the pilot and the surfer Dave mentions in his book, you'll find yourself in a steady groove that, with a little effort, you can keep going throughout your life.

Physics shows us that a perpetual motion machine can never be achieved, no matter how many people have dreamed of inventing such a device. But as Dave shows us, *perpetual motivation* is not just a dream—it has transformed the lives of countless people already. Why not let it work for you as well?

—The Editor

PERPETUAL
MOTIVATION

"Motivation will almost always beat mere talent."

—Norman A. Augustine

Introduction

The first step toward becoming more motivated is to notice the trap people often fall into. You want to become more motivated, but you think that you need more motivation to become motivated. It seems like a no-win solution: "How do I get motivated enough to become more motivated?"

It's a fair question. But the answer may surprise you. Motivation is not the same as effort. You may think—or feel—something like this: "To *be* five times more motivated, I'd have to *try* five times harder than I do now."

No wonder motivation is so hard to find! When unmotivated people look at someone who is highly motivated, they often give up quickly, thinking they just don't have what it takes to live a highly motivated life. In the pits of demotivation, thousands of mentally capable and physically healthy born-and-raised Americans are adrift in their own country.

Compare them to someone like Hiroaki Aoki, who immigrated to the U.S. before mastering English. This tremendous disadvantage demotivated millions of immigrants before him. But Rocky Aoki set about making his dreams come true in spite of the challenges he faced. Motivated to work seven days a week selling ice cream in New York City, he slept in storerooms to save money on rent. By saving and borrowing, Rocky scraped together enough money to finance his first four-table restaurant in New York. Now his international Benihana chain has served over 100 million meals, and he is wealthy far beyond the dreams of that struggling young immigrant. Sure, Rocky had a unique food service concept and great timing, but it would have amounted to nothing if he had lacked motivation.

Many people exert enough energy in life to get big results, but they don't focus their energies well. It's like trying to lift a heavy object—you can attempt to lift it with brute strength and a lot of sweat, or you can use a lever to make the task easier. Strategy and focus are your levers; they help you move the heavy things in life more easily. Highly motivated people know this; they are able to focus on the areas of their life that will fuel additional motivation and give their efforts tremendous leverage.

We all know highly motivated people, and we also

know highly unmotivated people. What makes these people so different? Which one are you? Or are you somewhere in the middle?

Some people seem to naturally have the inner drive to handle all of life's responsibilities and to achieve success. What motivates them? Are they different from you in some fundamental way?

Here's the secret: motivated people aren't any different from you. They weren't born with magic genes and high energy; they don't have any special facts at their disposal. So, what *do* they have?

The secret: motivated people aren't any different from you.

Formula for Perpetual Motivation

For over fifteen years, I've studied what motivates people. I worked with thousands of businesspeople, a host of athletes, many parents, and scores of children. I also looked at what worked in my own life.

As each year passed, I felt closer to answering the question: "What motivates people?" As my knowledge grew, I was able to help more people tap into their own capacity for motivating themselves. By developing and focusing on key ideas, we can all learn to be the type of person who has the inner drive to get the most out of life.

Now, finally, fifteen years after I began my research, I am confident that the following formula can act as a lever to enormously enhance your life through the power of motivation. Here is the Formula for Motivation.

Motivation *equals*

The Pursuit of Life's Perfect **Balance**

plus Integrity-Based **Influence**

plus **Creativity and Humor**

minus Runaway **Self-Esteem**

or

Motivation = B + I + (C + H) − RSE

With its several components, the Formula for Motivation is far more powerful than the popular two-word admonition, *be positive*. As does much of the material published today on the subject of motivation, *be positive* greatly oversimplifies the solution of the basic problem: How do I motivate myself to begin with, and, once motivated, how can I be sure I will stay motivated for the rest of my life?

It would be nice if the Formula for Motivation had fewer components, but it does not. Each component is essential, and each relies on the other parts. Motivated living is like a well-tooled engine. If one part isn't working, the whole engine can't function properly and might break down completely. Likewise, even if a person possesses all the components for motivation except one, the person won't be fully effective. He'll be like a new Mercedes with an oil leak, and his motivation to put forth continued effort will be weak.

Throughout this book, we'll look at the formula in more detail. Take a moment to look over the components, and ask yourself, "Do they apply to me?" Many people will find that they lack an essential component. Or you might find yourself saying, "I have everything the formula includes. I'm funny, a good communicator, well-balanced, humble, and very creative. Yet I'm not very motivated." Though you have all the parts, you haven't learned to put them together; you're an engine that hasn't been assembled yet. You might already be a motivated person, but you want to take your motivation to a higher level. This book will help you take that next step.

Throughout this book I will explain what is involved in each of the Formula for Motivation's components. You will come to understand how incorporating these concepts into your daily lifestyle will develop and maintain your motivation.

At first you may think the Formula for Motivation does not come naturally; as with any training, you will have to make some adjustments. But the more you weave the formula into your way of life, the more you will realize how natural it really is. Motivation is our natural way of being.

Legacy Achievers

During my many years of training people and researching success principles, I have come across a select group of people who excel through outstanding personal motivation. These motivated people usually leave a great impression on others. People remember a motivated individual long after an event, an accomplishment, even a lifetime. I call people who achieve the highest level of motivation *legacy achievers*, their legacy demonstrating the power of motivation.

I am not a scientist or a psychologist. But I have ob-
served literally thousands of people, and I took more than
15 years to crystallize a fully developed and teachable action philosophy about achieving and sustaining motivation. That being said, there are countless studies that
support the hypotheses in this book. The empirical data
resulting from these studies focus on the relationship between activities that are work-related and not work-
related. In this book I'll spare you the technical wording
and statistical overviews, but keep in mind that the information is at the ready if you are curious to learn more.

To simplify the material, throughout this book I portray
legacy achievers as though they all think, talk, behave, and
believe exactly the same things. Obviously everyone varies
in their philosophies and actions. Nevertheless, in basic
things, legacy achievers as a group have much in common. In many different ways, they all embody the effectiveness of the Formula for Motivation given above. They
are ideal examples of highly motivated and well-balanced
people.

Legacy achievers are able to achieve success in their
professional as well as in all aspects of their personal
lives. They balance the priorities and responsibilities of
family, finances, health, social contributions, faith, and careers. With these in balance, success follows and happiness abounds. There are many well-known legacy
achievers in the world, such as best-selling author
Stephen Covey or the late Mother Theresa. Who are the
legacy achievers in your life?

My parents, my grandmother, my first-grade teacher,
one of my insurance agents, several business-people I

work with, and many other people come to mind as the legacy achievers in my life. These people's lives have impacted others not because they are famous but because they have an uncommon peace about them. Their examples are compelling even when their lessons contain no words. Legacy achievers build reputations, generate motivation, and enjoy the experience of success. Imagine such a life—fulfillment beyond your wildest dreams.

The examples of legacy achievers are compelling even when their lessons contain no words.

While legacy achievers are not the focus of this book—I offer other material that discusses them in greater detail—they are important because they are terrific examples of motivation raised to a very high level. We have no better examples of the possibility for achievement in all our lives.

Perpetual Motivation

Being motivated is easy, but staying motivated is not. Think about it. How often have you said to yourself with great conviction, "My goal is to lose weight, and I'm starting right now"?

Or, "I'm going to be the number one salesperson."

Or, "I'm going to be the best manager."

Or, "I'm going to be the best parent in the world."

You're truly motivated at that time. It may last only a few seconds. But for those few seconds, you are highly motivated.

Through my research, I wanted to learn what happens between those inspired seconds and the next moment

MOTIVATION = Balance + Influence + (Creativity + Humor) – Runaway Self-Esteem when you find yourself uninspired, demotivated, and actually feeling negative about losing weight, being a great salesperson, or becoming a better parent.

I learned that the answer to sustaining the initial big bang of motivation isn't found in the sexy pat phrases we usually look for such as, "Think big," or "You've got to believe to achieve." I found a much more practical answer in the Formula for Motivation, an answer that always works in spite of any discouragement.

Since the formula includes several elements, each of which is crucial, we need to focus on every component to develop the motivation that leads to success. Often with math formulas, it's necessary to begin at the end of the equation; likewise with the Formula for Motivation we begin with runaway self-esteem, the last component in the formula. Understanding runaway self-esteem will make many of the other components easy to grasp and put into effect in our lives.

PART ONE

Ego and Balance

Pride escapes no one. It simply masquerades itself in order to go undetected. The greater its subtlety, the greater its power.

Runaway Self-Esteem

If you use a mirror for your windshield, sooner or later you will crash. You can boost your ability to motivate yourself by looking beyond yourself and focusing on others. Perpetual motivation requires you to purge yourself of the need to build up your self-esteem.

It is important to note that to live a perpetually motivated life, you must consider your life in its entirety, not just in terms of how it supports you. Some people simply look at their bank accounts or trophy shelves to take stock of their motivational track record. But the health of your interior life is the proper measuring stick. If you fail to consider broken relationships, a guilty conscience, and self-justifications, you can deceive yourself. External factors may report accurately your ability to generate results in certain areas of your life, especially those areas you enjoy, but truly motivated people master their entire person both inside and out. That is why the formula for motivation defined in the introduction emphasizes both.

Disregarding our self-esteem contradicts what most of us have been taught. At face value, self-esteem—meaning a *positive self-image*—is good. Here's the problem: while much of the material on building self-esteem is effective for living a fulfilling and motivated life, it's contaminated by half-truths and destructive advice finely woven through the constructive ideas. The harmful material is hard to detect. Reading this chapter will help you identify the common dangers found in self-esteem materials that actually destroy our motivation.

Unfortunately, today's concept of self-esteem often leads to self-worship, which is toxic for a healthy interior life. We are inundated with the importance of having high self-esteem. Self-esteem has become an overvalued solution to our various problems. Book after book tells us that a high self-esteem *produces* positive results and behavior in life. This is like spending money you don't have in the hope that you will earn it. In reality, healthy self-esteem is the *result* of positive behaviors, accomplishments, and/or honoring predefined standards. Whenever you focus on building self-esteem as the solution to your problems, you put the cart before the horse. This approach is both ineffective and destructive. Focusing on amplifying your self-esteem causes what I call runaway self-esteem (RSE).

If you cross over the very fine line of healthy self-esteem, you enter into selfishness and become self-centered.

Human nature has an automatic tendency to focus on self. It needs no encouragement. Adding fuel to the fire is dangerous.

Legacy achievers—persons who maintain perpetual motivation and achieve in all areas of their lives—receive so much fulfillment from focusing on important things outside their own skins that they have no need to focus on themselves. Legacy achievers get more done in a shorter period of time than most people. To boot, they use much less effort. They live with a clean conscience, master their own weaknesses, and soar with their strengths. They are the people in life who go beyond the "one hit wonder" phase and churn out platinum recordings year after year without fail. They live selfless lives yet can be found in various circles of life wearing titles such as CEO, All-star athlete, mom, dad, servant, politician, and actor. The list goes on.

Runaway self-esteem takes a negative toll on every aspect of your life and thereby destroys your motivation. The following presents various life issues briefly and the impact runaway self-esteem can have on them. Let's compare a person who has no need to build self-esteem (a legacy achiever) with a person focused on their self-esteem.

FAMILY~

When a legacy achiever father wakes up in the middle of the night to the sound of his baby crying, he focuses on the baby and his wife, not on himself. If he were to focus on himself, he would conclude, "Getting up would not be fair to myself. I have to go to work in the morning, and I got up the last time."

Instead, he thinks about how much his wife, who never gets a spare moment during the day, could use the sleep. He thinks about how the baby is uncomfortable and needs to be changed. When the focus is not on ourselves, the act of helping others is easier.

CAREER~

When a legacy achiever is at work, she thinks about helping the company perform better by doing her job to the best of her ability. When in a leadership role, this person focuses on developing the people she leads to be the best employee they can be.

A legacy achiever feels a sense of accomplishment when watching each of her subordinates mature. As a result, a legacy achiever's division grows and she is a likely contender for a pay raise or promotion.

People who are focused on themselves think about how much overtime they have worked, about how their extra efforts go unrecognized. They feel that Karen in the office across the hall gets more recognition and more perks than they do, even though her numbers are about the same.

This person thinks about how they could make more money at XYZ company, where they would be appreciated. As a result, they often jump from job to job. They are equally unhappy everywhere; their brief stays provide no opportunities for advancement; and their resumes soon reveal a pattern of job-hopping that eliminates them from consideration by many companies.

FINANCES~

When a legacy achiever handles money, he thinks about what a privilege it is to have the money in the first place. He thinks about the responsibilities that come with it and invests it wisely for the future. He also gives some of it back, contributing to charities and various worthwhile endeavors. If he were to focus on himself, he would spend the money primarily on items that would enhance his self-image or hoard it as a way to measure self-worth.

FAITH~

When a legacy achiever focuses on faith, she is governed not by her own opinions and pleasures, but by God's laws. When she is faced with an ethical or moral decision, she asks herself whether the outcome of her actions would please or offend God. People who are focused on themselves chooses whatever action suits them best, as long as they could get away with it.

HEALTH~

When a legacy achiever faces health issues and concerns, he chooses to eat properly and exercise because his health plays a powerful role in the lives of the people around him. He respects his body as a gift from God, put in his care. Someone who is focused on himself may take better care of material gifts than he does of his own body. Someone else, also focused on himself, may go overboard and worship his body with excessive care in search of a more impressive self-image.

MOTIVATION = Balance + Influence + (Creativity + Humor) – **Runaway Self-Esteem**

SOCIAL CONTRIBUTIONS~

A legacy achiever focuses on how past role models helped shape him throughout the years. As a result, he contributes to social causes from which he might not receive a direct earthly reward. Someone who is focused on himself does not donate time, money, or talent without considering what he would get in return.

The Greatest Problem with Self-Esteem Is the *Self* Part

In a conversation with Dr. Ray Guarendi, a well-known radio host, lecturer and psychologist, I was intrigued when he said that self-esteem was a late twentieth century concoction. I was already researching self-esteem, though I hadn't taken a close look at its roots. Sure enough, authors did not pay attention to self-esteem before the middle of the twentieth century. For the most part, early authors presented self-esteem as a result of behavior. Later authors present self-esteem as a means to behavior.

The notion that you need to run around engulfed in self-love would have appalled most people as recently as fifty years ago. Today magazines glorifying *self* fly off magazine racks; people buy products with "because I'm worth it!" tag lines. Our society has become wrapped up in the delusion of self.

The notion that we need to run around engulfed in self-love would have appalled most people as recently as fifty years ago.

Consider this popular self-esteem-building exercise: Look in the mirror every day and say twenty times, "I like myself. I like myself." All your problems should disappear. Don't count on it.

In reality, you may have good reason for not liking yourself. Therefore, you may not buy into building your self-esteem by lying to yourself. To suggest that you must like yourself prior to changing the behavior that has been preventing you from liking yourself is foolish and simply doesn't work.

Yet this easy-way-out solution epitomizes pop culture today. Prior to the recent flood of self-love, people found esteem in other aspects of their life. People measured self-worth through their family, relationship with God, and moral lifestyle.

The Universal Standards of Natural Laws

Today, many people base their self-esteem on pop culture ideals—without the counsel of moral truth.

The race for self-esteem starts at home. Overpraising children has become part of the culture of enhanced self-esteem. Many therapists and counselors are beginning to recognize the dangers in this. The November 22, 1999, edition of the *London Free Press* quoted Cheryl Noble-MacGregor, a child and family therapist for the Institute for Family Living, as saying: "Excessive praise becomes empty praise. It seems we are worshipping the god of self-esteem these days."

Many parents sell self-love to their children by suggesting, "Love yourself just because you're you." However, this circular logic demands no accountability. It means that children do not need to act, talk, or behave according to any set standard in order to feel good about who they are. Rather, when children are young, they need to be given

MOTIVATION = Balance + Influence + (Creativity + Humor) – **Runaway Self-Esteem**

some external perspective that will ground their sense of self-worth.

An example of a foundational standard could be something as simple—yet as important—as being taught that they are children of God. This can provide a solid footing, allowing the child to obey the natural law of right and wrong. This helps them to recognize their value even when their behavior doesn't reflect it. Natural laws are preset, external standards. Though they often don't agree with our opinions or desires, they always affect our well-being.

Advice to ignore moral standards and the universal standards of natural law is readily found on bookshelves. Typical of this advice is best-selling author Nathaniel Branden's book *How to Raise Your Self-Esteem*. Dr Branden writes in his summary:

"If we are to protect our self-esteem, we need to know how to assess appropriately our own behavior. This includes, *first, being certain that the standards by which we judge are truly our own, and not merely values of others to which we feel obligated to pay lip service.*" (Emphasis added.)

At face value, this sounds like advice I might give my children when other kids try to influence them, such as by taking drugs in order to be cool. I might say, "Don't pay attention to what those kids are doing; do what you know is right." The difference between my intention and Branden's intention is uncovered when you understand his definition of *others*, which is "country, family, state, the true faith, society, and more."

In contrast, I might tell my child to do what he "knows is right" because he *does* reflect learned values, having learned what is right and what is wrong from his mom and dad. Since Branden's followers are taught to disregard family and societal standards, a child would decide to take drugs based on whether he thought it would hurt or help his perceptions of himself.

Branden devotes an entire chapter to teaching disregard of what most people call unselfish standards. Not only is this an ineffective solution to a problem, it's also destructive.

When a child is not given a benchmark for earning self-respect and instead sets his own self-esteem standards, the effects can be harmful. It is similar to a child making up all the rules at home in place of his parents. If this were the case, he would undoubtedly proclaim: "I get candy any time I want, and I get to go to bed as late as I want."

Independent standards for self-worth, with no regard for others, would shove established standards aside. The child could not know how damaging the long-term effects of this would be.

If employees practiced this philosophy, they would disregard their leadership's standards for performance. Instead of feeling good about accomplishing company performance expectations, Branden's disciples would make up their own standards. Anyone who has ever held a leadership position will tell you the employee-set standard is generally lower and much less effective than the company standard.

The idea of personal standards has already infiltrated the educational system. In some schools students even grade themselves!

Too many people in society live by this independent

standard philosophy; as a result, they fail to pay taxes, steal from their neighbors, and even kill people. All because it fits into their selfish perspective.

In fairness to Dr. Branden, he does provide some very sound advice. It's advice I would give others and have learned from myself. In fact, a thorough reading of his books shows that Dr. Branden believes: "We cannot work on self-esteem directly, neither our own nor anyone else's, because self-esteem is a *consequence*—such as that of living consciously, responsibly, purposefully, and with integrity. If we understand what those practices are we can commit to initiating them within ourselves and to dealing with others in such a way as to *facilitate* or *encourage* them to do likewise." (*The Power of Self-Esteem*) I agree with this statement. But the theme of independent standards found elsewhere in his materials can be disturbing and destructive because it contradicts this sound advice.

Dr. Branden talks about the importance of responsibility, living purposefully, having morals and integrity, and parents setting boundaries for their children. My question is, how does a person arrive at what is responsible, moral, or purposeful if they are told to disregard others (as defined earlier) when developing their own standards for self-esteem? Dr. Branden cannibalizes his own advice for his readers by providing these two very opposite perspectives.

Dr. Catherine Cardinal also extols the popular notion of personal standards in her book *The Ten Commandments of Self-Esteem* (Andrews McMeel Publishing). The first commandment she lists is: "Thou shalt not consort with people that make thee feel bad about thyself." Dr. Cardinal explains that if we associate with people who make us feel bad about ourselves, we should leave the relationship, even if we have been in the relationship for some time.

Dr. Cardinal fails to suggest that people might actually have a good reason for feeling bad about themselves when in the company of certain individuals. Suppose a business partner of mine showed up at an important meeting unprepared. He should feel bad with that group of people because feeling bad is the appropriate response to his acting irresponsibly. Feeling bad is often what triggers us to improve.

Dr. Cardinal's advice would apparently be to quit the job and go where others are also unprepared, so you don't have to feel bad about your own behavior. I don't really believe Dr. Cardinal or Dr. Branden would tell someone to quit their job in this situation, but some people interpret self-esteem material as an all-encompassing self-preservation technique.

Therein lies the problem. Too much self-esteem material lets us off the hook without our having to change the behavior that makes us feel bad in the first place. Whatever happened to the good old saying, "You should be ashamed of yourself"?

> *Too much self-esteem material lets us off the hook.*

When you take away external standards, you take away the target—perpetual motivation to live a good, successful life. If you set our own self-esteem standards without considering preset family, social, church, and company standards, to name a few, you risk walking through life aimlessly, stripped of a significant source of our motivation. If you play basketball without baskets, hockey without goals, and

MOTIVATION = Balance + Influence + (Creativity + Humor) – **Runaway Self-Esteem**

baseball without diamonds, you will endlessly bicker about who won or lost.

Setting standards for measuring your success without considering external standards is like people saying, "I want to believe what I want to believe." This is a common but foolish desire. For example, I'd like to believe that eating cheeseburgers and ice cream while lounging on the couch will make me look like Arnold Schwarzenegger. But my desire to believe that does not change reality. If my desire was my only resource for health and fitness, I would never become healthy.

The reality that governs how your body responds to your diet and level of physical activity is a law of nature. Likewise you need external standards to determine whether or not your self-esteem is substantiated.

Outside standards such as the Laws of Nature are analogous to the universal standards of Natural Law. Natural law, a preset, universal standard, often doesn't agree with your feelings or desires but always affects your well being and squares with what you deep down know to be true about yourself.

There is some confusion about the difference between Natural Law and the Laws of Nature. *Laws of nature* reflect that gravity is real and that we are subject to its effects. It is a law that subjects your body to a new wardrobe when it consumes excessive calories and exerts no energy.

Then there is *natural law*, which also affects motivation. Natural law is the innate law, universally present in the hearts of all people. It is the foundation of most judicial systems. It tells people, from a logical perspective, based on human nature, that some things are just wrong—such as, that it is wrong for you to take what is not yours. Or, better understood by some, it is wrong for me to take what is *rightfully* yours. It is the innate law that enables you to use the word "rightfully" in the first place.

Natural law is what tells you that inducing physical harm on defenseless people is wrong. You don't say it is "not good" to hurt innocent people—you say it is *wrong*. You say that because you know it to be true at your core. Certainly there are people who have warped their consciences to the degree that they ignore natural law, but that is an unnatural mentality. In extreme cases this is easy for us to see.

Clearly all rational beings condemn the behavior of Stalin and Hitler but subtle breeches of natural law are more difficult to identify, especially for people who haven't trained their conscience. This is true because at the center of all breeches against natural law is pride. And pride is blinding.

As it pertains to motivation, the pursuit of self-esteem is a breech against natural law because the fuel for self-esteem is excessive pride; this takes away your ability to grow—why grow, why change at all, when you don't even admit that you have any shortcomings?

Natural law and the Laws of Nature govern in a similar fashion. They act as excellent analogies for each other. And both are beyond refutation. No matter how badly we might sometimes want to believe they do not apply to us, they do. For example, if I acted upon a sincere belief that I could breathe water rather than air, I would die. It would not matter how sincere my belief was.

You need to investigate what laws of nature exist in the

world and operate in concert with them. That doesn't mean you need to consider *all* external standards when determining your self-worth. Obviously many individuals, groups, and organizations believe in different standards. You must determine which of these standards are consistent with natural law and your objectives in life before you decide to accept or reject them.

If these standards are in harmony with natural law, you can accept them and be confident that they will not come back to hurt your motivation, impair your self-image, or endanger your survival.

When explaining this topic, I once used the analogy that when we decide to fly with a certain airline, we also decide to trust their standards. But when we walk down the Jetway, if the aircraft we're supposed to board looks like a bathtub with plastic wings, the airline's obvious failure to understand the laws of nature regarding flight would instantly destroy our confidence in them. As a result, we would reject the airline's standards because they were not in accordance with the laws of nature that refer to aerial navigation.

A woman disagreed with my analogy, saying the Wright brothers couldn't have invented flight without challenging the laws of nature. "It's not natural for people to fly," she maintained.

However, she misunderstood. The Wright brothers were not trying to defy a natural law, they were trying to understand it and work with it. A greater understanding of the laws of gravity, the physics of thrust and lift, and the principles of controlling flight—in other words, submitting to these laws and operating within its limits—made flight possible. Only when these laws are defied does an airplane crash.

Let's bring the analogy back from the laws of nature to the natural law. In our daily lives, when we operate within natural laws we can discover new thrills, but if we defy natural laws we will crash.

The tough question is, how do we know what all of the natural laws are? This ultimately becomes a religious debate. While this book touches upon some aspects of faith, it was not written to provide a theological or philosophical explanation of the genesis of natural law. Although this information is not provided, it's important to recognize the need—in our professional lives as well as our private lives—to seek the truth and to abide by it once it has been found.

Self-Esteem Is Selfish Steam

As I grew up, I felt terrible about my actions when they did not meet my parents' standards. That feeling motivated me to make changes so I could feel good about how I behaved. I never felt hopeless or unloved. I always knew that my parents loved me unconditionally. However, my parents spent more time teaching me to respect others than to worry about myself.

Today many parents are worried about making their children perpet-

Respect begets respect.

ually happy rather than respectful, responsible, or productive. The latter goals usually mean short term discomfort but long term effectiveness. One reason is that when we treat others with respect, they tend to treat us with respect also. Respect begets respect, which creates a motivated atmosphere at work and at play. As a result, we gain a sense of self-respect that sufficiently fills our need for self–esteem.

Today, however, many people teach kids to regard themselves with higher esteem than anyone else in the world. Is it any wonder that some teachers report today's students as acting with less respect for authority than in the past? Why not? We send them into the world as selfish people. Filled with *selfish steam.*

We should be doing just the opposite. We should teach children the value of standards, order, and discipline to better function outside themselves. They must be taught that serving and respecting others is honorable. How does this relate to you?

We all go through stages in life when we wear moral or logical blindfolds. It takes maturity and wisdom gained through living to unveil our ignorance. We can all relate to the feeling of embarrassed enlightenment we have experienced when our ignorance was exposed. To elaborate on these blindfolds we all wear, let's look at a typical child.

An eighteen-month-old who cries when prevented from playing with a burning candle does not see the danger in the activity. No matter how you try to caution the child, he thinks being deprived of the fun is unfair.

In just a few short years, when the child is five years old, he can see the logic behind the action—his blindfold has been removed. However, new blindfolds have replaced it. These new blindfolds prevent the child from seeing the reasons for limiting his consumption of junk foods or setting a bedtime.

Life experience and a measure of maturity gained by the time the child is fifteen can make his old perspectives about bedtimes and junk food seem funny to him. His blindfolds on those issues have long been removed, but he now wears a new one. This blindfold covers his understanding of why his parents won't let him go to a party on Saturday night. At this age, it may seem as if this blindfold is strapped to his face rather than loosely tied to it. For the life of him, he cannot understand why his parents are so strict about a simple party. This blindfold may remain until he has his own fifteen-year-old son, but eventually, as he matures, it will come off.

The point is, we all wear self-centered blindfolds at one time or another. You probably have one or more on right now. If you do not seek counsel from people other than yourself, you may never remove the blindfolds holding you back. These blindfolds can be very personal and may include issues related to self-esteem. Sometimes the blindfolds that we wear prevent us from growing or changing our own behavior.

The Packaging Does Not Change the Contents

The accepted popularity of attaining *self*-esteem mangles the moral fiber of our society. This warped emphasis on *self*-esteem blurs the foundation for motivation. No matter how well people package self-esteem, the package holds selfishness.

Some people ask me, "Dave, if you're right about our

culture's overreliance on self-esteem, how did the topic become so popular?"

There are two primary reasons for this popularity. First, it's a seductive concept that people want to believe. Second, writers such as Dr. Nathaniel Branden state things like, "I cannot remember a time when I did not perceive this doctrine (re: "living for others," "obedience," and "selflessness") disastrous for mental and emotional well being." (*How to Raise Your Self-Esteem*).

Such opinions appeal to people. They validate our own selfishness. When people can reference a book, with a doctor's name on it, to bolster their reasons for being selfish, they will. Some people claim that their selfishness is an honorable thing to pursue, in the name of their own well-being. People who have bought into pop culture's glorified self-esteem philosophy often defend it vehemently. That philosophy is their shield against being called selfish, and they know it.

Some psychologists claim a scientific connection between self-esteem and results. However, the variables they chose to include or omit affect—and in some cases have largely determined—the results of their studies. The same argument, of course, can be used to reject studies I find more credible. Nevertheless, numerous studies reveal few, if any, connections between focusing on self-esteem and results, whether it's good grades, cultural prosperity, or job performance. If there were a connection, it would more accurately be defined as a connection between self-confidence and results. Self-confidence is not derived from an internal pep talk. It is the result of training, education, and a track record of results.

A study done by Professor Bruce Ryan at the University of Guelph, in Canada, showed that the effects of behaviors, for fourth through seventh graders—such as acting out, internalizing problems, peer sociability, and rule compliance— were completely irrelevant to self-esteem. In a conversation I had with Professor Ryan, he exclaimed, "The most powerful factors for predicting academic success are intellectual effectiveness and academic effort."

On February 5, 1990, *Time Magazine* published an article about a standardized math test that was given to thirteen-year-olds in six different countries. The test included the statement "I am good at mathematics." The students were to answer yes or no as to whether or not that statement described them personally. The American students scored the worst on the math portion of the test but ranked the highest on the question related to self-esteem. Sixty-eight percent of the American students felt they were good at math.

The philosophy of the importance of self-esteem has penetrated our society to an astonishing degree, as shown by the math study question. Our young people had the worst scores but the greatest self-esteem. They operate under a delusion, comical if it didn't indicate such dire consequences for both the individual students and our nation. Fostered by the ideal of self-esteem, our young children believe a falsehood: if they think they're good at math, they are, regardless of their test results.

Even Dr. Branden would not classify these children as having healthy self-esteem. He commented on the *Time* article, saying, "One of the characteristics of people with

healthy self-esteem is that they tend to assess their abilities and accomplishments realistically, neither denying nor
exaggerating them." (*The Power of Self-Esteem*, Dr. Branden Health Communications Inc., page 34)

Here we have a problem again. How are these children
supposed to assess their own "abilities or accomplishments" when they are told to disregard outside standards
as well as people who make them feel bad? There's only
one answer. They *must* consider the standards of others if
they are to accurately assess themselves.

Union of Esteem

According to the National Center for Health Statistics, the
divorce rate nearly doubled from mid 1960s to the mid
1990s. I find the correlation between the climbing divorce
rate and the concurrent societal shift toward the importance of self-esteem during the last half-century very interesting. To me, the relationship is telling: The greater our
focus on *self*, the higher the divorce rate.

Many marital problems stem from selfishness. An unfaithful person puts his or her libido ahead of marriage.
The person who uses financial problems as an excuse for
divorce covets money over marriage.

There is little to no room for focusing on self in marriage. Rather, a person must consider marriage a *union of
esteem*. A union of esteem refers to loving the couple you
become in marriage more than yourself.

Think of the powerful symbol of lighting the Unity candle at a wedding. The bride and groom pick up two candles at the altar, which represent the two individuals. The

two flames are united into one larger flame. Then the couple extinguishes the individual candles, which represented themselves singly.

I remember the story of a man who asked a pastor on the night of his rehearsal, "Which side of the altar do I walk around after we light the Unity candle?"

"That's easy," the pastor replied. "You go where she goes. From that point forward, you are one!"

The most challenging time in my marriage came just after the birth of our first child. When Kevin arrived, my wife and I, as do many new parents, felt stripped of every spare moment. I would come home from work and think, "I need a break." Lisa would see me come home from work and think she deserved a break. This was miserable. It was not until we put each other's needs first that we found peace and, as a result, wonderful and powerful motivation. Today we have six children, and the effort and emotional energy that it takes to manage the household with all six is less than it was when we only had one.

A person focused on self in marriage does not serve the marriage. If you come home from work like I did, tired and irritable, you too may feel that you deserve a break. But your spouse may have had an even worse day. If you are focused on yourself, your spouse may not have the opportunity to share with you his or her own situation. If the kids need your help, the bills need to be paid, and your in-laws are coming for a visit next week, tension can rise and resentment can build.

This is when people start feeling sorry for themselves. It's also when we get nitpicky about who has done what. "I did the dishes last night; you should do them tonight."

MOTIVATION = Balance + Influence + (Creativity + Humor) − **Runaway Self-Esteem**

Or, "Can't you just *one* time help get the kids in bed?"
Soon we start keeping track of who did what, and our
focus on ourselves reduces us to acting like an overtired
three year-old.

On the other hand, a couple focusing on serving their
marriage as a unit attends to each other. The desire for
service to one's self disappears. When one partner needs
the support of the other, that partner pitches in to help. A
union of esteem evolves.

Too often so-called marriage counselors take a "what-
are-you-being-deprived-of" approach to counseling couples. This is like helping a couple fill out divorce papers.
If you focus on yourself, you will never be satisfied. An
effective solution helps the marriage partners focus on
serving each other, which is rewarding in two ways.
First, each partner gets an incredible feeling from will-
fully doing for others. Second, when two people serve
each other, both people also receive service in kind.
Therefore they no longer feel needy.

A misplaced desire for self-esteem destroys the purity
of motivation. Even major league baseball suffers from
runaway self-esteem. Team loyalty
suffers as a result. Today, free agency
helps players get more money year
after year, placing the focus on the individual, not on the team. Self-loyalty
replaces fan loyalty, coach loyalty, and town loyalty. Unfortunately, the nature of the game is also changed because
many players measure their self-esteem by the size of
their contract, not by contributing to a winning team.

A misplaced desire for self-esteem destroys the purity of motivation.

As I mentioned earlier, companies also suffer the cost of

rampant self-esteem. If an employee needs daily assurance that he or she is the greatest and doesn't get a daily pat on the back, that person may quit and look for appreciation and praise elsewhere.

It's okay to *like* recognition as an employee. However, employees who *need* recognition all the time usually don't become legacy achievers. In fact, employees driven by self-esteem often self-destruct. No one prospers from an *appreciate-me-or-I-quit* attitude.

That internal philosophy holds true for people in leadership roles, too. Leaders preoccupied with self-esteem inevitably make decisions motivated by selfish agendas. Selfish agendas hurt the (external) organization.

Suppose Phil Jackson, coach of the incomparable Chicago Bulls during the 1990s, craved more personal glory for the team's success than star player Michael Jordan was receiving. Think of the destructive moves the coach might have made if he had focused on himself instead of the team. Instead, Phil Jackson shined the light out onto Michael and the other Bulls to create a cohesive team—a team that responded to the coach.

Putting others first will give you an indescribable feeling of exhilaration. Life gets easier when you focus on family, friends, church, vocation, and others instead of yourself.

This philosophy may sound contrary to popular books that push selfish concepts, including the bestseller *Looking Out for Number One*. This book mocks the idea of putting others first. Furthermore, I challenge you to find a happy, successful person whose main focus is on himself or building his self-esteem. After all, the greatest way

MOTIVATION = Balance + Influence + (Creativity + Humor) – **Runaway Self-Esteem**

to diminish your ability to motivate yourself is to focus on yourself.

The entertainment industry is loaded with successful people who need alcohol or drugs to get through the night. As a result, many of today's stars are killing themselves with drug overdoses or alcoholism. Years ago, two of the most famous actors of their time, William Holden and Richard Burton, succumbed to alcohol. More recently, John Belushi and Chris Farley used the same combination of cocaine and morphine, both accidentally ending their lives at age thirty-three. The number of similar cases in the entertainment industry is too long to list here.

There are also many exceptions. Michael Caine won't shoot a film on location unless his family can be with him so he can make sure they are safe and comfortable. Celine Dion and her husband, after battling his cancer into remission together, renewed their marriage vows and, at the pinnacle of her success, she has temporarily retired to spend more time with him and realize her hopes for children.

Paul Newman, who was also troubled by the realities of celebrity, found better ways than drugs to come to terms with fame and riches. He used his name recognition to build a highly successful food company that donates all of its after-tax profits to charities. Since some aspects of celebrity made Newman uncomfortable—especially its tendency to exalt the recipient's self-esteem—he focused its power on others through his food company and his charities. Mel Gibson has spoken many times of the destructive lifestyle he lived early in his career. Accolades such as being *People* magazine's Sexiest Man Alive turned his focus onto himself, and he regrets hurting the most important people in his life during those days. He knew that making *The Passion* could be career suicide, but he decided to commit his talent to works that dealt with themes bigger than who he was personally.

Celebrities who lack this moral foundation often ask themselves, "Is this all there is?" and drift into searching for motivation. Ironically, the joy and self-respect people gain by focusing on others instead of themselves is exactly what people focused on building self-esteem crave but never get.

The Eye of the Beholder—
Self-Esteem and Appearance

As mentioned before, self-esteem can't be determined solely by your own independent standards. But this doesn't mean your personal opinions don't have a role in determining how you feel about yourself. They do. What people say about us often influences how we feel about ourselves. If a young person is told they're ugly by someone they respect, they may start believing it. This is sad and can have a brutal effect on their perception of themselves over the years.

Yet someone else who is told they're beautiful by someone they respect may still insist they are not. In fact, they may feel distressed by their personal appearance. Ugly and beautiful are matters of taste. If a person's taste conflicts with their own physical appearance, it will be extremely difficult to convince them that they are attractive. And it's a mistake to tell them they must see themselves as physically beautiful. This will encourage them to spend excessive time examining their personal appearance, which they have already decided is ugly.

Focusing on unchangeable things that we don't like about ourselves—such as our height, facial shape, or bone structure—is futile. Rather, focusing on things that we can change about ourselves makes more sense. Obviously, we can change some of our physical attributes such as our hairstyle, and even our weight only to a certain degree.

I know people who are convinced they are ugly and have high self-esteem. I have also known people who are convinced they are physically beautiful, yet have low self-esteem. Logically speaking, the only conclusion to these observations is that our appearance is not the deciding factor in our self-esteem.

We have all seen television commercials promising to restore your hair "but more importantly your self-esteem." Does loss of hair equate to a loss of self-esteem? Certainly not to all bald men. In fact, Michael Jordan chose to shave his head to appear bald. I doubt that he was deciding to remove his self-esteem.

If we try to convince someone they are physically beautiful when they don't believe they are, we will never succeed. Think of your own experiences trying to do so. Sometimes we can't even convince a person that *we* think they are beautiful. Trying to get a person to believe they are beautiful when they are simply not wired to believe it will not work. This is like trying to convince someone who doesn't like liver that it's a taste treat. No matter how many times they try it, they still don't like it. No pep talk to themselves in the mirror can change their perception. There is only one positive step for a person in this situation: focus on inner beauty and on outside factors rather than on oneself.

In high school I had an acne problem. I thought that made me ugly. No one on the planet then or now could convince me otherwise. When I thought about my acne, I shut down socially. In other words, I lost my motivation to be active and engaged. But when I took the focus off my face and put it on the activities I was doing or the people I was with, my personality would change. I became more confident and outgoing.

Taking the focus off myself resolved my self-esteem problem. I did not look in the mirror and try to convince myself that I liked my appearance. I did not say "I am a handsome young man" twenty times each morning in order to convince myself that the acne wasn't there. I just stopped focusing on what I could not change.

> *Taking the focus off ourselves resolves our self-esteem problem.*

Serving Ourselves and Others

Does all this talk about serving others mean we don't spend any time on ourselves? Certainly not. To do so would mean neglecting ourselves, which would make us ineffective at serving those around us. You must make time for yourself, investing in your attitude and ability, which will enhance your motivation to support important causes.

For example, Brett Favre, long-time quarterback of the Green Bay Packers and three times the National Football League's Most Valuable Player, works hard at developing his throwing arm. He watches his diet and studies game films. He spends this time investing in himself, and both he and his team benefit. By maintaining and further developing his individual skills, he fulfills his obligation to serve his team.

If his motivation to do this were only to glorify himself or to secure a better contract, he would cloud his motivation and it would hurt his performance as well as the team's results. In the same way, a paramedic is not being selfish when he or she spends extra time learning better life-saving techniques. This is an investment in time for the good of others. A paramedic who takes a break from the action to go golfing invests this time as a means to refocus. Likewise, a mother may spend a night out with the ladies in order to relax and then refocus on her family. None of this is selfish if it is done for the right reasons.

We all need to take some time to develop our own attitudes or just plain relax in order to be effective. We just need to pay close attention to our purpose for doing so.

One Step Further

Some of the signs of runaway self-esteem are obvious—especially when we notice the signs in other people! But one trap of self-esteem that can catch us off-guard is the desire for self-justification.

MOTIVATION = Balance + Influence + (Creativity + Humor) − **Runaway Self-Esteem**

Avoiding the Trap of Self-Justification

The most powerful motivators of all are virtue and vice. This might seem like a surprising thing to say. It would take an entire book to look at all the ways this is true, but let's look at a single vice, one that's closely tied to runaway self-esteem—*self-justification*.

I can't begin to count how often I have witnessed people who are otherwise unmotivated become powerhouses of persuasion, leadership, and military excellence due to the second-strongest motivator of all—*self-justification*.

I often educate my clients on the impact that self-justification has in the workplace. When I point out that it's the second-strongest motivator, they can't help asking:

What is the number one strongest motivator? I usually ask them to guess, and the most common replies are "fear" and "hate." Thankfully something does triumph those two motivators—*love*. Luckily, fear and hate typically have short-term value. Eventually, fear usually turns to exhaustion and hate to self-destruction, which diminishes the power of the one who hates. But even when these motivators keep their power, they can be trumped by love.

Virtually every workplace study supports this fact, but in simple terms we can know this based on common sense and experience. A mother who is fearful of alligators would dive into a lake with an alligator in it to save her child. Likewise, a man who hates his boss would keep his job to provide for his family.

But let's get back to the second-strongest motivator of all: self-justification. Self-justification is the essence of pride and self-deceit. Self-justification can be defined as the intentional mental altering of reality (and truth) in an attempt to conform the world to our own weaknesses and shortcomings. Most people do this to some extent, because, at least in the short term, the pain associated with admitting one's weakness or errors seems too great; we'd rather live a lie.

Sales managers and parents both have a keen ability to recognize self-justification. Sales managers who have advanced through the sales ranks because of their strong work ethic often find themselves listening to sales reps offering a long list of excuses for poor results. Of course, legitimate reasons for poor performance exist in sales, but people close to the profession know that the true reasons are smothered by the countless excuses. Failing reps will explain that the economy has changed, that clients no longer value the products, that the competition is too intense to succeed. On the same day, sometimes even during the same meeting, other reps, who sell the same products to the same clients, will talk about how easy it was for them to close accounts. It takes an intuitive manager to determine whether the failing rep lacks skill and training, or if he simply has the wrong attitude and disposition to be in that role. If the rep has the right training, skills, and disposition, but still provides excuse after excuse about the outside factors affecting his results, he is probably trapped in a mode of self-justification.

Mothers and fathers know this truth as well. Many parents have listened to their son or daughter provide excuses for poor results or behavior in school. At the same time, they see the child excelling in his or her hobbies and interests. When it comes to hobbies, a child may diligently pay attention to instructions and work in a timely manner to attain goals. Clearly, then, the child doesn't lack an ability to plan well. Committed parents recognize the importance of teaching their children to apply the same level of focus to school work.

Losing Motivation

If not corrected, the student and the sales rep suffer the same agonizing demise. They lose motivation. This happens in one of two ways. The first is when the person drenched in self-justification is so motivated to make his poor behavior acceptable and "right" in the eyes of others that he spends endless time and energy defending his

MOTIVATION = Balance + Influence + (Creativity + Humor) − **Runaway Self-Esteem**

wrongness. This is especially tragic when the person is actually aware that he is wrong. Unfortunately for him, there is an inevitable end of the road. At some point he must face his weaknesses and admit that he was wrong. The further down the path of poor behavior he travels, the more difficult it will be for him to face reality.

There are many surprising aspects to a person who uses self-justification as a motivator. One, discussed earlier, is that he fails to see that he is motivated by self-justification. Even more fascinating is how many resources he will employ in an attempt to advance his cause. He becomes more creative than he has ever been! He mentally jumps through endless hoops in order to see things his way and help others see things his way, even when he knows it's just a mirage. He operates from an emotional subjective perspective, but he weaves in random arguments that sound like objective logic.

He sometimes recruits others who may suffer from the same poor behavior. It is commonly understood in sales that negative people spend more time recruiting others to become negative than they do prospecting for customers. When the self-justifier is able to recruit an ally, he becomes more committed to his cause. He does not say, "I am right because the empirical data demonstrates this." He instead says, "I am right because Bob agrees with me." This is a perfect place to insert the timeless wisdom that two wrongs (or even a hundred wrongs) don't make a right. They only distract a person from reaching his or her own potential, which can only happen when he enters the world of truth and reality.

The second negative consequence of self-justification as

it relates to motivation is *shut down*. A self-justifier's inner and outer dialogues can lead him to depressed behavior or even genuine clinical depression. When you fight an inner battle between what you know to be true and what you wish to be true, it's a losing cause, and exhaustion sets in.

As with pride, the antidote for self-justification is humility. Pride blinds all of us. If you are frustrated by watching other people accomplish things that you know you could accomplish, but always find an excuse to avoid, then take a look at the pride you have in your life. Humble yourself to seek the truth about your performance, lack of commitment, behavior, and attitude. You will probably find that a reduction in pride and an elevation in humility will give you clarity and perspective that was blinded by your pride. Your new humility, fueled by clarity. may be just the catalyst that you've always sought but never found. The results will follow.

Evaluating Your Conscience

Of course, it's hard to admit that you have a problem, precisely because self-justification feeds off of self-delusion. It's like going to a class wearing a blindfold and earplugs, but claiming to be paying attention. Your only shot at getting past this handicap is to evaluate your conscience at its deepest level.

This is why the self-quiz in the chapter on self-esteem can help you take the next step. Yes, *you*! Don't fool yourself into believing that you're exempt from this exercise. There is hardly a person alive today who is not, to some degree, a victim of his own self-justification. Here are some key questions to think about:

1. Are you failing to reach your financial goals because you are justifying your poor spending or investment habits?

2. Are you failing in your relationships because you are not at the service of others, yet at the same time you're too demanding?

3. Are you compromising your integrity in order to get ahead?

4. Do you need to justify the words, actions, and motives you use to earn money?

5. Are you overly critical of other people who have the same weaknesses you have, acting as if you are appalled by their actions?

6. Are you disorganized with your time and bad about meeting deadlines, but consistently blaming others for your failures?

7. Do you use weak excuses to justify your lack of charitable contributions?

8. Are you harboring resentment toward others for past transgressions against you?

9. Are you moving from one job to the next because in every situation, you believe "the company" or "the boss" treated you wrong?

If you flinched or felt a little embarrassed while you read this list, then consider examining in a deeper way the cause of your anxiety. No doubt this may be the most liberating and empowering solution to your motivational challenges. Get in tune with what you know to be true about yourself—even when the truth isn't pleasant to observe—and you will kick your results into high gear. What changes do you need to make in your life to free yourself from self-justification in all of its forms?

I mentioned earlier that a person in the state of self-justification is operating primarily from an emotional perspective. It is worth coming back to that idea. Emotions are good; in fact, they can be great! They make up the zest of life, but they must be controlled in order to be constructive and beneficial. Therefore emotions can't be the method by which you set your flight path for life. You must use logic to set the direction of your motivation and *then* *fuel* the logic with your emotions. If you choose to set a direction based on emotions, you will fly out of control—think of a 747 jet engine unconnected to an airplane and with no one to direct it. The power is ferocious, but nothing good comes of the power. Conversely, if you set your direction based on logic or objective thought, but you fail to add the fuel of emotion, then you will lack the passion and power to overcome obstacles needed for success—you'll never lift off.

We must be courageous but also reasonable.
The world admires us for walking a
tightrope without falling off. It asks us
to keep our balance.

—Lech Walesa

The Pursuit of Life's Perfect Balance

Balance in life generates motivation, leading directly to success. This conviction comes both from my research and my experience. Over the past seventeen years that I have spent in business as an executive and consultant, I've been absolutely amazed at the relevance of the topic of balance. Many authors who write on the topic do so to help people feel fulfilled, happy, or less stressed.

Those are worthy goals, and the material in this book will help you attain them, but the topic here is motivation. You should understand that this topic of balance as it relates to motivation in life is not a cotton-candy, feel-good platitude. It's entirely relevant. Early in my career, I tried to help people with the traditional motivational techniques. I trained people with all the best self-help, positive-attitude information on the market, but I found there was something bigger than that working against me. It was the forces in life that define people beyond who they are at work. Little by little I discovered that if I helped people get more control of the issues that were unrelated to their actual job, they performed better and needed less job-based advice. In other words, they already knew how to do their jobs, but acted as if they didn't because the other factors in their lives clouded their ability to perform and think clearly.

In other words, I found myself becoming what we now call a business coach. At the time there was no such popularized name so it felt more like being a counselor.

The topics of motivation and life balance are very personal to me. Like all of us, I am pulled in many different directions every day. One major benefit of researching and writing this book has been the opportunity to test my own motivation as well as to practice my balance skills.

I try to live in the manner presented in these pages— the key word being *try*. In pursuit of this goal, I continuously work to improve my own life despite setbacks and failures ranging from mildly disappointing to very painful ones. Ultimately, however, every setback and failure I experience equips me with greater motivational skills. Knowing this helps me get through every crisis more quickly and with less damage.

Whether you consider yourself highly motivated or highly unmotivated, you'll be able to better your life through the examples set for us by legacy achievers. I will share examples of how legacy achievers focus on balance throughout this chapter.

Motivation results from the successful pursuit of life's perfect balance. So what is *balance*? Webster defines balance as *mental or emotional stability*. But those are not easy to attain. From my research and experience, I've learned that we all need to balance six significant points in order to feel mentally and emotionally stable in life. Whether or not you're aware of them, everyone's life includes these six key balance points. There are many other aspects of life, of course, but none are as important as the six; whether they use this exact language or not, all legacy achievers focus on them, and so can you. The six balance points are:

- ~ Family
- ~ Financial responsibility
- ~ Health
- ~ Social contribution
- ~ Education and vocation (*knowledge in motion)*
- ~ Faith

Balance Is about Engaging

Balance is not about avoiding, it's about doing. Balance is about engaging in a pursuit and meeting challenges rather than dodging them. Often the worst response we can make in a situation is to do nothing.

Consider one example we all know about. Some people try to balance their health by avoiding fatty foods and sugar. That's a good start. But unless they eat healthy

MOTIVATION = **Balance** + Influence + (Creativity + Humor) − Runaway Self-Esteem food, as well as exercising regularly, they aren't going to find balance in their health.

Here's another example. Some people might say, "I want to get my life in balance by spending more time with my family." Excellent idea. But when they do spend more time at home with their family, all they do is watch television instead of talking or playing. To pursue life's perfect balance, you need to engage in activities that bring your family closer together. This can be as simple and cost free as going outside and playing catch with your children, or as complicated and expensive as taking your family skiing, sailing, or rafting down the Colorado River.

Some things appear active but really aren't. Someone may decide, "I need to get in balance financially, so I'm going to clip coupons." That's fine, but unless they invest wisely to make their money grow, it's not enough to attain balance.

Thus, the pursuit of balance has two aspects: a negative and a positive element. The positive element—taking action—is the most important for most people. The negative element—avoiding certain things—is somewhat less important. (One exception is for people who are fighting some kind of addiction. In their case, avoidance of their particular poison is one of the most positive things they can do.)

Balance Equals Energy, Effort, and Focus

To gain life's perfect balance, we cannot merely divide a twenty-four day by the six balance points. Gaining balance is not only about time. It's also about energy. Effort. Focus.

Even if you need to work ten hours a day, by exerting energy, effort, and focus on the other balance points, you can even things out and bring balance to your life. Maintaining balance takes energy and contemplation, but the effort pays off in peace of mind. Conversely, if you fall off balance, every other part of your life suffers.

Spinning the Plates

Maintaining life's perfect balance is like a performer spinning plates at the circus. He puts a plate on a long stick and spins it, balancing it as he sets up another stick. Then he spins a second plate, then goes back to give the first plate a boost. Then he adds another plate, and another. It only works if he goes back to keep the other plates spinning, otherwise they wobble and eventually crash.

How many plates can he spin at one time?

Now think of your own life. Dealing with the six balance points is like having six plates to spin. Our six plates are family, finances, health, social contribution, education and vocation, and faith. Just like the circus performer, you need to continually give each plate at least a little attention—a tweak now and then—to keep it spinning smoothly.

If you have only one focus in life—perhaps your career ambitions—it may consume most of your time and energy. You might find yourself thinking along these lines: "To be brutally honest, I like this plate a lot more than any of the others, so I'm just going to keep on spinning it, and let the others take care of themselves."

For a little while, the other plates keep spinning via

their momentum, but if ignored for a long time they'll begin to wobble. Sooner or later (usually sooner), they'll fall and shatter.

Spinning plates provide a powerful visual image of the focus and effort you need to put into each of life's balance points. If you neglect any given plate, it wobbles and eventually falls. And then the crash. It could be a broken marriage or a financial crisis. When this happens, you need to glue the pieces back together. Let two or three points fail, and the difficulties can seem insurmountable. The repair task is never impossible, but it will take more time and demand more effort than if you had just kept the points in balance in the first place.

If your time is used sincerely, thoughtfully, and energetically, it takes little time to maintain spin on any of the plates you're tempted to neglect.

To maintain balance, you need to educate yourself about all six of life's balance points. You need to attend to each of the balance points every day, giving each one a quick twirl or heavy attention, as needed. It takes a bit of work, but this is the inescapable necessity and joy of living a satisfying, highly motivated, balanced life.

And the good news is this. When you get in the habit of giving all six balance points a little tweak, a little added spin, every day, it doesn't feel overwhelming. Only when you let one or more of the plates start to wobble and fall do you really feel overwhelmed and out of control.

You may see the six points and say, "Hey, you forgot golf—leisure time helps keep me balanced." Well, spending time on hobbies and personal interests is fine, but if it comes before balancing the relevant points in life, you're falling into a trap. Putting your participation in golf or some other pastime ahead of life-balancing points inevitably disrupts your life's balance. As your out-of-balance life wobbles, your friendships, family, and career begin to suffer.

Researchers would call what I have been talking about *spillover* or *congruence*. Studies have shown that the relationship between work and family life can have a building, cross-relational effect. They also show that the troubled areas of our lives can negatively affect a plate or balance point, even one that seems to be completely unconnected to the trouble at hand. In other words, any time one of the plates falls, it can negatively affect another, and any time it spins gracefully, it can have a positive effect. (Edwards and Rothbard, 2000)

You may coast through life out of balance for some time, but eventually your plates will start to fall.

My point is not that golf inflicts trauma, although sometimes it feels that way to me personally. Rather, favoring priorities outside the six balance points usually ends in disaster. You may coast through life out of balance for some time, but eventually your plates will start to fall. Then you are left with nothing but broken pieces.

Another crucial point is this. Balanced people find great joy in hobbies such as golf or just plain goofing off. When you life is in balance, you actually find *more* time to enjoy other activities than when you are out of balance. In fact, mixing hobbies and other favorite activities into your balance points can be incredibly rewarding. But the balance points have to be the priority.

You need to educate yourself in order to understand the real value of the six balance points. You need to know how they work together. If you concentrate on balance every day you will generate motivation, and it will guide you to success.

Of course, some days you can't be physically present to spin all the plates in person. If you travel all day, it may be impossible to spend time with your children or with your spouse—but chances are you can phone home. With cellular phones, what could be easier? Maybe you can't be there for your daughter's dance recital. When something like this happens, you need to spin the family plate again to move back into balance. The key point here is to know how long you can be away before you lose the ability and strength to regain what is currently out of balance.

In addition to a phone call or spinning the family plate a bit harder when you know you'll be away, it's also important to act in a way that honors your family position and name. If your behavior is reckless, even if you don't get "caught," you'll strain your interior life and soon experience a decline in motivation. I have seen this many times. In fact, Las Vegas has identified it to such an extent that one of their promotional themes is, "What happens in Vegas stays in Vegas." The entire city's economic "health" is based upon people lowering their moral standards while they stay in Vegas. Sadly, this promotion works, and the result is strained or broken relationships for the people who buy into this.

The Six Balance Points

Let's take a closer look at each balance point.

FAMILY ~

Today's technology allows us to get things done faster, go places quicker, and communicate more widely than ever before. Yet families are also more out of touch than ever before.

The family dinner has been replaced by the fast-food drive-through on the way to soccer practice. Live, in-person, role models have been replaced by fictitious television characters with oversexed and easily outclassed personalities.

The number of sensible parents who monitor what their children watch on TV has been overtaken by the number of parents who let the tail wag the dog at home. Many parents justify letting their preteen children watch violence and sexually explicit content by saying, "What are we to do? They like it."

For many of our middle-class citizens, the American Dream once meant having a white picket fence around a home filled with two loving spouses and happy, well-mannered children. But for many people today, that dream has been replaced by today's reality: a security fence around a massive house half-filled by what's left of a broken or dysfunctional family, its rooms stuffed with expensive status-displaying gadgets.

This is the sad picture of many American households today, and a major part of the problem is the growing lack of balance in our culture. When you put your work and finances ahead of your family, sometimes even by telling yourself it's for their own good, you do grave damage to yourself as well as to the people around you. The ramifications of such a tragic lack of balance destroys your ability to focus. This in turn destroys your ability to be motivated and eventually ends in disaster.

Understanding how to balance the important responsibilities you have to your family with the rest of your non-work life is crucial to your well-being. You can find abundant joy and a source of true motivation in your family relationships.

The challenge is that this sometimes requires forgiveness and healing. No matter what your family situation is, if you harbor resentment and un-forgiveness, you are operating at a lower level than you are probably aware. It takes very little time to forgive someone, and the result can be liberating. This is one of the most simple and powerful ways to increase your ability to live a motivated life.

Forgiveness and freeing yourself of resentment are not things you need to know *how* to do, they are things you must be *willing* to do. If you are harboring these feelings in order to punish another party, it is important to know that you are the one who is being hurt the most. You will increase your level of motivation and joy immediately upon letting go of these destructive vices.

Although we are talking about family, it's important to remember that each balance point affects all the others. For example, if parents neglect to discipline their child— when the youngster's behavior cries out for discipline— and continue this neglect for a long time, they can be sure of the consequences. The child will grow into an undisciplined young adult who will likely get into trouble as a direct result of not being appropriately disciplined when young and impressionable.

When trouble of this kind comes calling, the parents are forced to respond. Depending on the situation, the ensuing stress could lead to difficulty in concentrating at work. Challenges at work are likely to have a financial impact on the family (financial responsibility balance point). To handle the stress, a parent might exercise less and eat more (health balance point). The resulting tension could lead to neglect of societal responsibilities (social contributions balance point). While these worldly matters are tearing at the parent's heart and mind, the person under stress may forget to ask for God's help (faith balance point). As a result, all the balance points fall victim to the original problem, which was neglecting family responsibilities.

Thus we need to keep a shared focus on each of the balance points. Thankfully, simple awareness of the six balance points is often all that many people need to start leading a balanced life. For others it takes a bit more.

We can learn a lot from two very important lessons taught by legacy achievers. First, a legacy achiever puts his or her family ahead of self. Second, legacy achievers look at families as no wimp clubs.

Putting Family First

Let's carry the philosophy I shared in the previous chapter further; that is, runaway self-esteem is a killer. When a family reaches the threshold of unbalance, the result can be divorce, or death of the family. Although not a positive topic for discussion, we can learn how to avoid this tragedy by looking at its cause.

Divorces are caused by selfishness. That may sound like a personal judgment, but it's not. Rather, it's a conclusion derived from talking to a large number of divorcees of both genders who have shared their stories. According to all of them, when they cut through the froth, selfishness was the basic reason their marriages broke up.

Further examination divided divorcees into three groups: the majority blame their ex-spouse's selfishness, a smaller group say both partners were selfish, and even fewer admit the breakup was caused primarily by their own selfishness. When we break down the trigger causes for divorce, it's easier to see this.

An unfaithful person puts his or her sexual desire ahead of the marriage. A couple divorcing for financial reasons puts material goods, services, or addictions ahead of family. Couples claiming to have fallen out of love selfishly stopped loving. Spousal abuse is caused by a selfish need for control or a selfish lack of control over temper. A workaholic selfishly puts his or her career ahead of family.

Other forms of selfishness supply even more subtle reasons for divorce. For example, communicating ineffectively can be a lack of willingness to learn about the other person, which is essentially a selfish attitude.

This is not to say that all these issues aren't difficult to handle—they are. I'm familiar with the stress that financial constraints can put on a marriage. At age twenty-four, I ran into a financial struggle as a result of being self-employed, which meant it could recur the following year.

My financial obligations included tens of thousands of dollars in short-term debt—plus car and mortgage payments—all piled up in one year.

My wife, Lisa, was not earning an income because she was staying home with our son, Kevin. To complicate matters, we were expecting our second child and did not have a maternity rider on our health insurance policy. Our insurance company refused the rider because Lisa's first delivery was a C-section, which cost them twenty-three thousand dollars. This meant we faced the possibility of additional hospital bills totaling that amount. I had to work harder than normal to make up the funds, which added to our stress at home. It was a tough year. We went through a lot of aspirin.

When I look back on our difficult year, I can see how being challenged by finances can hurt a relationship. But I can also see how those challenges create an opportunity to grow as a family. Lisa and I took the opportunity to reaffirm the commitments we made to each other before we married. Due to our own positive childhood experiences, we decided that we would live in a tent and ride bikes before we would send our children to day care. We actually used those words to paint a picture of the priorities in our lives prior to our wedding. When the financial strain hit, the unwanted challenge was an opportunity to stay true to our commitment. The whole situation, teaching the lesson of balance, became a positive experience in our lives.

Challenges create an opportunity to grow as a family.

Taking the focus off ourselves and putting it on the needs of our children provided us with a sense of security.

Knowing what was really important to us allowed both of us to focus on our individual responsibilities to the family. With our perseverance and pursuit of balance, including faith in God, we were able to conquer the financial challenge in the following months and years.

For many people, divorce is not a concern. The commitment to their vows—for richer or poorer, for better or worse, in sickness and in health—never wavers. For these people, the challenge may be in finding happiness in the marriage to which they have committed. Couples throughout the world who have found happiness, discovered it by serving the members of their family. These people have discovered the value of taking the focus off themselves and putting it on others. Through their unselfishness, they actually receive more from their families than do selfish individuals who try to get the family to focus on them.

Some people become nervous when they hear about legacy achievers putting their families first. They feel for themselves, for example, that such an attitude might compromise their work performance. However, as we mentioned earlier, legacy achievers are the employees that companies pursue. Their personal life is in order, and as a result they can concentrate effectively and creatively at work. They register fewer sick days and can even put in overtime when necessary because they don't have to worry about plates falling down around them.

A person who routinely neglects their family responsibility is put under tremendous pressure when they need to commit extra hours at work. The decision to stay longer at work may mean a long-unspun plate will finally fall. When out-of-balance people are asked to work overtime, they face a much greater decision than does a legacy achiever. The unbalanced person may be forced to choose between family and work.

A Happy Family Is a No Wimps Club

With privileges come responsibilities, as every legacy achiever understands. Meeting responsibilities involves sacrifices. Making sacrifices means no wimping out. In marriage, you must be willing to face any accompanying difficulties. Abandoning a problem is not a solution—it simply creates a greater problem. When your children are disobedient, it takes effort to discipline them. But failure to discipline them always creates even tougher problems.

Too often these days, parents are afraid to discipline their children. This fear leads to a lack of balance in the lives of every family member.

It begins when the children are very young. A toddler is given whatever he wants because he creates a ruckus if he isn't satisfied. Fearing a scene, the parents cave in and meet the child's demands. When the child is older, bigger, and louder, the parent's discomfort will escalate. The youngster, who now believes he can get everything he wants simply by being nasty, will be almost impossible to please.

Without doubt , there are valid reasons to dread children. Lisa and I have four children and hope for more. Having a martial arts background, I have been in the ring against men as large as six feet five inches and 309 pounds. None of them had the chutzpa my four-year-old son has. At the moment he stands about two feet ten inches high and weighs thirty-eight pounds, but he has more drive in him than any ten of those men.

My son's commitment to getting what he wants is amazing. When he was three years old, he went through a bad phase including throwing cereal bowls and temper tantrums lasting up to an hour at decibel levels that would have made The Who wear earplugs. Not having gone through this with our other children, Lisa and I wondered where we had gone wrong with this son.

When my parents witnessed his temperament, they didn't respond with the same concern we felt. In fact, they laughed!

My mom said, "Dave, now you know exactly how *you* acted when you were three years old." They then provided counsel on how to correct the problem.

With our improved perspective, Lisa and I set out on an intense corrective program. We had to be brave enough, and persistent enough, to address every single rebellious action. It also demanded plenty of energy for the essential follow-through. Envisioning our child down the road, twice as large and twice as loud, provided some inspiration to stay committed. But the thought of how miserable his life would be if he did not learn to control himself was the real motivation behind our determination to control his defiance. Thankfully, our son has moved past this behavior and although he occasionally tests the old behavior, he quickly realizes his objectionable actions get him nowhere. Today he controls his emotions much better and, as he has always done, makes me smile every day.

You may wonder what this has to do with motivation.

Consider what Dr Ray Guarendi says: "To discipline your child without love is cruel, but to love you child without discipline is child abuse." He explains that if you don't discipline a child when he is young, then when he is older, the school principal, police officer, judge, or drill sergeant eventually will. The personal strain that takes place when family issues arise can be enough to set parents back financially, physically, and spiritually, not to mention professionally.

A husband who wants to improve his communication with his wife must be brave enough to deal with the necessary effort. A wife who feels the need to fix her husband's ways must also be courageous enough to let go of her perspective. Children must also face responsibility. They must be brave in disclosing the truth to their parents about the mistakes they have made.

Families are definitely No Wimps Clubs. They take real fortitude, patience, and love. Remember, balance is about engaging in actions; it doesn't come from avoiding difficult situations. To find balance, fearful parents, a husband who lacks communication skills, a wife who wants to change her husband, and demanding children all need to have the courage to engage in difficult thoughts and actions.

You must remain strong to handle life's difficulties. This is not always easy, especially when it seems you are faced with thirty-six-hours' worth of things to do in a twenty-four-hour day.

Sometimes you need to make tough choices. If a choice compromises your family's well-being, it is the wrong one. If it serves your family, you'll never regret it.

FINANCIAL RESPONSIBILITY ~

Money is only good for the good that it does.

—Martin Domitrovich

Financial responsibility means something different to each of us. We often associate money with emotions. Some people experience varied levels of self-esteem, happiness, sadness, jealousy, greed, generosity, distress, excitement, failure, and success all due to money-related matters. Money can generate an equal number of positive and negative emotions.

Sometimes the idea of balancing our finances can be overwhelming. Our society sends us many mixed messages about money. Some people live by this philosophy: since you can't take it with you, you might just as well spend it as fast as you get it. Other people, suffering from an even greater lack of self-control, take it a step further and spend money before they earn it. In contrast, some people go to the opposite extreme and hoard money as a means of security.

What is a favorable perspective on how to handle wealth? Legacy achievers have a tremendous perspective on money and, not surprisingly, their perspective is balanced. Legacy achievers enjoy a portion of their money today while they save some for tomorrow. Meanwhile, they donate to worthy causes.

Money is not the only way legacy achievers measure earthly wealth.

But money is not the only way legacy achievers measure earthly wealth. Time, talent, and relationships are priceless assets.

I gained a great perspective about money from a

legacy achiever named Marty Domitrovich. He said, "Money is only good for the good it does." This attitude is commonplace in the lives of most legacy achievers. A story he told me about himself illustrated that he meant what he said. Marty met his wife, Katie, in the late 1960s when he worked as an in-the-home knife, pot, and pan salesperson. Katie's father liked Marty but objected strenuously to his daughter marrying a "door-to-door knife salesman."

Katie's father even refused to attend their wedding because he did not approve of a marriage "doomed to be burdened by financial ruin," as he put it. This upset Marty and Katie very much. Marty was filled with negative feelings for his father-in-law that he knew would bring no good to his life. He knew he had to turn the negative emotions into something constructive for the good of his family.

He privately made a commitment to himself to earn enough money in the knife business to donate more to a charity than his father-in-law made in a year. He did this not out of anger, but to turn his father-in-law's lack of faith into a positive incentive.

A number of years later, Marty made good on his promise and donated the money. I'll never forget the sound of accomplishment in his voice when he told me this story. But he never told his father-in-law, nor did he strain the relationship by holding a grudge. Marty's constructive goal allowed less fortunate people to benefit from what was initially a negative circumstance.

Legacy achievers do not view being rich or being poor

as either good or bad. Rather, they look at the way people handle their money as a measure of their character.

Legacy achievers do not always choose lucrative careers. These people demonstrate their character and maturity by living within their means and, despite not having a lot of money, still contribute their time and talent to worthy causes.

Many legacy achievers with more financial flexibility are careful to keep materialism at bay. They are conscious that money itself is okay, but "the love of money is a root of all kinds of evil." (1 Timothy 6:10 NIV)

To keep our lives in balance we need to balance our finances. When we experience financial pressures, our judgment can become clouded. It's important to become educated about money and engage in actions that will allow us to help ourselves and others financially.

HEALTH ~

*Good health is something that makes you
feel it's a fine day when it isn't.*

—Anonymous

Legacy achievers are motivated to stay healthy because they know their ill health could have a detrimental impact on those who are close to them. If your health were to fail, it could put tremendous burdens on your family and others who care about you. Life deals enough challenges without neglect helping them along. Therefore, it makes sense for you to avoid tragedy or careless health habits whenever possible. Healthy choices are a great way to do this.

Just as neglecting your family and your finances can have a domino effect on other balance points, so too can your health. Balancing your health and well-being can be both complicated and simple. Being constantly bombarded with sales pitches regarding good health that appeal to our egos and any tempting hedonistic impulses we may harbor complicate our health choices. However, some basic principles have passed the test of time and are readily available for your use in simplifying your health care.

First, we must acknowledge that we will never find the key to better health exclusively in: a fad diet, foods currently considered healthy, an exercise regime, or vitamins or supplements.

These are fleeting, one-dimensional solutions. Rather, a relatively healthy person will find the key to good health by combining the following four ingredients: a reasonable diet, routine exercise, controlled stress, and monitored risks.

People who live motivated lives have energy. If the spirit is willing but the flesh is weak, then often the things you want to accomplish in life will never be attempted. I have seen many people get caught up in the latest fad to the degree that it practically becomes a religion. But legacy achievers are the people who take a common-sense approach to their health on the positives (what to eat and do) and on the negatives (what to avoid eating and doing).

Maintain a Reasonable Diet

Every so often a new weight-reduction philosophy takes America by storm. During the 1960s, the popular solution was to avoid starches. In the 1970s, avoiding sugar was stressed. During the 1980s and 1990s, avoiding fat was paramount. The Atkins diet, which has been around for years, recently gained popularity. This diet does not restrict fat, but does limit carbohydrates.

You can find people who claim each of these fad diets is the be-all and end-all answer to good health. You can also find people who claim to have tried these diets with no success.

The problem with most of us today is that we are looking for a magic solution to great health—as long as it's effortless. Most people who live long, healthy lives do not stay committed to any extreme diet or quick fix. Rather, they eat reasonably throughout their lives.

Exercise Routinely

Just eating properly won't give us balanced good health. A study published by the *American Journal of Clinical Nutrition* showed that 90 percent of people who lose weight and keep it off also exercise at least thirty minutes four times a week.

The Institute for Aerobics Research in Dallas, Texas, found that people who don't exercise have poorer attitudes toward food than do people who exercise. Sedentary people tend to think healthy food is boring, difficult to find, and too time consuming to prepare. However, adopting healthy eating habits, when combined with adequate exercise, will improve our attitude about food. A good attitude enhances motivation.

Exercise may also reduce the odds of developing deadly diseases, including heart-related problems and cancer.

Some studies indicate that athletes are more than 50 percent less likely to develop certain diseases than nonathletes. A report published in *The New England Journal of Medicine* relates that middle-aged men reduce the risk of developing diabetes by 6 percent for every five hundred calories burned by exercising weekly.

Exercise is also the most significant way to slow the aging process. Our bodies contain a substance called human growth hormone (HGH). Once we reach our twenties, naturally released amounts of HGH start to decline. Scientists say that reversing the aging process requires the release of more HGH. Exercise does this. When you exercise, natural HGH pours into your system, which probably explains why many people who work out look younger than their counterparts who don't exercise.

Control Stress

A third major health factor is controlling stress. Excess stress may cause tremendous physical and emotional health problems. Both appropriate diet and exercise help control stress, but you can do more. Consider the following two commonalties among legacy achievers when it comes to handling stress.

1. Get Enough Sleep
   Easy tasks are hard to handle when you're tired. Sometimes we refuse to admit we're tired. This may be a carryover from childhood. When children become crabby, parents know they may simply be tired, although the children will deny it emphatically. Adults often have the same reaction to

MOTIVATION = **Balance** + Influence + (Creativity + Humor) – Runaway Self-Esteem

fatigue. We too become crabby. Unfortunately, we are a lot bigger and a lot louder,
and no one can make us go to bed. (On the
other hand, too much sleep can also make
you lethargic. The bottom line is to get
enough sleep but not too much.)

2. Face the Problems
Another good way to reduce stress is to face
our problems head on. This is consistent
with engaging in action as opposed to avoidance in order to find balance. Researchers
at Southern Methodist University in Dallas
believe we can improve our immune system
and increase our sense of well-being by taking the time to actually write down our worries. Writing down worries makes the
problems more tangible and thus more
under our control. This activity allows us to
view and understand our problems in a con-
crete manner.

The general nature of the relationship between stress
and illness has long been known to the medical world.
Some doctors believe stress and feeling a loss of control
may double our chance of catching the common cold because these emotions can reduce the effectiveness of the
immune system. Therefore, facing our problems is extremely important in controlling stress.

Monitor Risks

Physical activities sometimes expose us to risks; therefore, you should carefully calculate what you choose to do and the consequences you may face as a result of your choices. However, you can't live in total fear, refusing to take part in any activity that presents some risk. You must simply think ahead and take precautions to guard your physical health.

If you were to live in constant fear of being hurt, you would most assuredly miss out on some great pleasures in life. Unfortunately, many things can cause us to fear various activities. For example, horseback-riding accidents put seventy thousand people a year in the hospital. It's enough to scare some people away from ever getting on a horse. But an isolated statistic may not tell the entire story. It's wise to find out all the facts before choosing to participate in or avoid life's pleasures.

Bowling injuries cause twenty-two thousand people a year to seek medical treatment. This news probably won't keep you out of the alleys if you enjoy bowling. However, this statistic does put horseback riding injuries into perspective.

You cannot be effective in life if you live with an excessive fear of taking risks. Likewise, you cannot be successful if you throw all caution to the wind. Once again, the secret lies in balancing your risks. You need to consider more than yourself when you calculate what activities you choose to undertake. This means carefully considering who is affected by the state of your health.

MOTIVATION = **Balance** + Influence + (Creativity + Humor) – Runaway Self-Esteem

SOCIAL CONTRIBUTIONS ~

Do something for somebody every day for
which you do not get paid.

—Albert Schweitzer

There seems to be a growing what's-in-it-for-me attitude in America today. Proof of this attitude's popularity is
illustrated by the heavy sales of a book titled *Looking Out*
for Number One.

The book was a bestseller for over a year, and, long
after its release, is still in demand. This book, which
mocks the idea of helping others, flew off the bookshelves.
For those of you who don't know, books sell mostly by
word of mouth, which means that many people loved the
I–Me concept in *Looking Out for Number One* and couldn't
wait to tell their friends about it.

The author, Robert J. Ringer, is articulate, intelligent,
and witty. He says people do things in their own best interest. This is generally true.

However, it's not absolute. The fact that people often
do things in their best interest does not mean the practice
is good. In reality, such a focus is often destructive and
can be a sign of weakness. When we
overcome this weakness, we will
strengthen our society enormously.

The fact that people often
do things in their best
interest does not mean the
practice is good.

Ringer believes the opposite. He
denies that people should ever do
anything from which they derive no
direct benefit. When a person does give without expecting
anything in return, he believes they are acting irrationally.
He says, "Simply stated, don't do something for the reason

that it's 'the right thing to do' if there is no benefit to be derived from it." This concept completely disregards natural law, charity, and family values, not to mention the principles of most major religions.

Do you suppose the people who recommended his book to their friends ever stopped to reflect on what kind of friend endorses such a concept? What would happen if your friends all bought into this concept on your moving day? What about when you get sick, need a ride to the airport, or just need someone to talk to?

Ringer goes well beyond preaching the importance of selfishness. He claims your standards should not be influenced by anyone but yourself. This is right in line with many of the self-esteem issues we discussed in chapter 1. He actually says there is no such thing as a moral right or wrong. "Your moral standards should be what you define them to be." He goes on to say, "just make sure *your head is on straight*." (Emphasis added.)

How do you know whether your head is on straight if you have nothing with which to compare its alignment? Ringer calls people who believe in natural law, in other words people who believe in right and wrong, moral absolutists. And he holds these people in such low regard that he actually categorizes them with violent criminals, thus leading us to suspect either that he nurses some serious hangovers from childhood or is simply aiming for shock effect.

Ringer also expresses low regard for rapists, murderers, and robbers, apparently not realizing how ironic this stance is. After all, violent criminals are only following his advice by determining their own moral code and looking out for number one.

The most impressive companies I have worked or interacted with embrace an attitude that is the complete opposite of looking out for number one. During a stay at the Walt Disney World Yacht and Beach Club Resort for a convention, I had an opportunity to witness staff perform many selfless acts, their personal social contributions to the workplace.

In one instance, I walked down what seemed like an endless hallway searching for the men's room. Having no idea where it was located, I must have looked somewhat confused. A gentleman vacuuming the carpet about forty yards away recognized my perplexity, stopped what he was doing, walked down the hall, asked what I needed, and pointed me in the right direction. He had nothing to gain by his actions, and I had not asked for his help. No supervisor was in sight, and he set himself behind a few moments in his own duties. His small act of thoughtfulness is commonplace with Disney employees.

During the same convention, I was the leadoff speaker one morning at 9:00 A.M. My assistant and I were puzzled about some of the information called for in my presentation. I needed to run back to my room five minutes before I went on stage. However, my room was located about ten minutes away by foot.

As I ran from the meeting room, I saw a gentleman transporting laundry on a golf cart. I was about to explain my situation to him, hoping to get a ride. But before I could get past, "I'm in a hurry," he pulled me into the cart and whisked me away to my room. In fact, he even took me through restricted back ways, saying, "Don't tell anyone I took you through here because customers are not allowed to see this area."

He too had nothing to gain from me or from any of his superiors. His social contribution and that of = the gentleman who helped me find the men's room were small examples of selflessness that added up to a mountain of service at Walt Disney World. If we could bring this attitude of social contribution into the workplace, onto the streets, and everywhere else in life, we would live in a wonderfully different world.

I don't want to live in a society where everyone is focused on looking out for number one. We all need help at some point in our lives. For some of us it's in the form of money, time, or emotional support. Some days we help others, knowing they will help us in turn. But you should also give of yourself freely, without any strings attached. Sure, you may still get something in return, but if you do, you should simply consider it a blessing and be grateful for it.

Societal contributions go way beyond donating to charities. The little things that you do every day add up and shape what society believes to be acceptable behavior. For example, drunk-driving statistics reflect the power of society's shifting views. Since 1982, fatalities related to drunk driving have fallen by 36 percent according to the MADD (Mothers Against Drunk Driving) Web site.

In considerable part, this is due to the initial efforts of one person, Candy Lightner. Candy's daughter, while walking along a city street, was killed by a drunk driver. Because of her motherly pain, Candy helped found MADD.

This organization's impact on the way our society views drunk driving has been incredibly effective and beneficial. Legislatures all across the United States have taken dramatic steps to discourage drunk driving because society now demands it.

The way you treat the checkout clerk, your waitress, or the driver who cuts you off on your way to work all add up.

It doesn't always take a large-scale contribution to society like Candy Lightner's to make a difference. The way you treat the checkout clerk, your waitress, or the driver who cuts you off on your way to work all add up too. In each instance, we are all part of the problem as well as part of the solution. If we want to change the world, we must begin by changing our own attitudes.

EDUCATION AND VOCATION (KNOWLEDGE IN MOTION) ~

I don't think much of a man who is not wiser today than he was yesterday.

—Abraham Lincoln

Education

One of the first mentors I had as a businessperson was a man named Don Freda. He is a successful leader and founded a very successful company. It was his responsibility, he taught me, to teach his team of executives everything he knew about his business. He realized this process would help his team grow and mature. If he ever achieved the goal of teaching his team everything he knew, he would no longer be able to serve them, he said. That was his motivation to continue to educate himself.

Freda's philosophy is consistent with an overriding

theme of this book, which is finding motivation through serving others. Instead of looking at continuing education as a way to build up his own self-esteem, Don saw it as a way to be effective in serving others. As a result, his business flourished. He developed a loyal following and did so without focusing on building his own self-esteem. I am grateful to Don for his lessons. They continue to serve me well.

Legacy achievers follow this same philosophy when it comes to continuing education. We must continually learn more to remain effective at our chosen career or vocation. Additional knowledge is a great motivator.

No matter what we do, we can always improve ourselves. Improvement is achieved through increasing knowledge and appropriately applying it. Education plays an important role in balance because every balance point is affected by knowledge. We can't eat right if we don't know what eating right means. We can't invest properly if we don't know how to invest. We can't have faith if we don't know what to put our faith in. We can't share with our family if we don't know what our family holds dear. And we can't help our neighbor if we don't know he's in need.

This section is subtitled "Knowledge in Motion." Knowledge rarely leads to prosperity if it's kept in a static state in our minds. Thousands of people have enough knowledge to be motivated and therefore successful, but they lack some element of the Formula for Motivation. As a result, their vast store of knowledge is out of proportion with their limited achievements.

These people are like a Ferrari motor inside a Pacer body. Because they lack part of the Formula for Motivation,

MOTIVATION = **Balance** + Influence + (Creativity + Humor) – Runaway Self-Esteem

they are not able to take full advantage of the motor underneath their hood. The reverse scenario also exists in the world. Some people have every component of the Formula for Motivation in the palm of their hand, but they lack the knowledge it takes to make the formula effective. These people are Ferrari bodies powered by Pacer engines. They can easily handle the turns ahead but lack the power to race forward.

It's important to continue educating yourself, for in no other way can you harness the full power of the formula for enhancing your life.

Vocation

What is a vocation? And how does it differ from a job or a career? A job is defined as follows:

> 1. *A regular activity performed in exchange for payment*, especially as one's trade, occupation, or profession
> 2. A position in which one is employed

A career has the following definition:

> A *chosen pursuit*; a profession or occupation.

A vocation is defined this way:

> A regular occupation, especially one for which a person is *particularly suited or qualified.*

(Source: dictionary.com. *Emphasis added*)

Simply put, a *job* is a way of exchanging work for money. This is not something that will sustain your motivation. The reward of money is not enough for most people, even the most money-hungry, to find fulfillment, and a lack of fulfillment leads to a lack of motivation.

A *career* has a greater chance of keeping you motivated, but it still falls short. Many people who choose a career choose it simply because they *want* to do it or because they *like* the activity. Wants and likes are great ways to choose your path in life, but they will fall short of fulfillment if you fail to consider the emphasis in the definition of *vocation*. Are you "particularly suited or qualified" for your chosen profession?

The desire to satisfy financial needs often gets people started on the wrong path in life. They make long-term concessions in order to meet immediate needs or wants. Sometimes this is necessary, but the longer people stay in a job the more difficult it is for them to break away from the routine, even if they lack motivation to work. It's like being in a relationship with a person you don't even like.

If you pursue your direction in life with a career mentality, it's highly likely that you won't perform as well as your peers. And even if you do, you won't find fulfillment—rather, you'll see your motivation decline rapidly. Michael Jordan followed his vocation when he played basketball, and he flourished. When he tried baseball, he slipped into career mode. He *liked* and *wanted* to play baseball, but he failed to consider that he simply wasn't up to the level of a pro player. His motivation faded as well, and he went back to basketball where he belonged.

If you choose your path in life based on vocation, you'll find fulfillment and sustained motivation. A vocation encompasses your temperament, natural talents, likes, and dislikes.

Choosing a vocation doesn't mean avoiding things that might not come easily to you, nor does it mean finding an ideal job that's free from all challenges or frustrations. There is no such thing as worthwhile work that is free from undesirable tasks. If you're the type of person who goes from job to job looking to avoid minor irritations, stop your search. Examine your gifts and pursue your vocation.

You'll know when you've found your true vocation because the undesirable tasks will be overshadowed by your vocations' mission or purpose . The problems won't magically vanish, but you won't concentrate on the problems because you'll be too focused on the objective. It's similar to a good marriage, where love sustains a couple even during hard times.

Try this self-quiz before turning to the next section.

1. I was first interested in my current job because: (salary, skill set, necessity for money, prestige, and so on.)
2. Three skills I have to offer my community and my world are:
3. Working within my current job, the two things I could change to be more vocation-oriented are:
4. Thinking about the long run, three things I can imagine doing that are vocation-oriented might be:

You will find gratification in pursuing what you were made to do. A Ferrari isn't made to carry grocery bags through suburban streets, and a minivan cannot achieve greatness on a race track. Each must do what it's designed for, or it will never reach its potential. Being on a path that takes advantage of your potential will sustain you when things are difficult because, believe it or not, the knowledge that you are not wasting your gifts is rewarding enough to pick yourself up, day in and day out.

FAITH ~

It takes a lot more faith to live this life
without faith than with it.

—Peter DeVries

Two of the most consistent traits found in legacy achievers are humility and peacefulness. Of course, they are not immune from pride or restlessness, but when these concerns rise in them, legacy achievers become resolute about making a correction. Consistently, the majority of legacy achievers point to their faith as the source of their peace even in the midst of outside turmoil and suffering. They see challenging times as opportunities to grow, and they attribute their faith as the source of power to overcome difficulties.

I have interviewed a significant number of highly successful people, who exercise nearly all the parts of the formula for motivation with the exception of one, faith. It may seem judgmental for me to omit them fromlegacy achiever status, but often, by their own admittance, they lack the peace found in legacy achievers who explore their faith. That lack of peace also affects their ability to sustain success in other areas of their lives.

MOTIVATION = **Balance** + Influence + (Creativity + Humor) – Runaway Self-Esteem

Legacy achievers are not all of one faith. They participate in different religions and subscribe to different beliefs. It may sound contradictory, but some legacy achievers claim that they are not sure whether God really does exist. But the common thread they all possess is a sincere desire to find out whether He does exist, and when they discover a new truth about Him they embrace it without reserve.

In other words, it is the desire to know what is true and the humbleness of heart to embrace the answer once it is discovered that makes someone a legacy achiever. You may ask, "What does this have to do with motivation?" It is simple. A clear conscience is motivating. Ignoring life's inevitable questions—"Where did I come from?" and "Where will I go after I die?"—sooner or later become a source of stress. You would not take the same approach with your checkbook and expect to find peace. Ignoring the balance because you don't think it is important or because you are afraid of the answer will not help. Eventually, the guilt that comes from ignoring the balance will wear on your motivation even if the banks don't get to you first. Human beings are spiritual creatures. We desire to know our origins. Young children are fascinated by stories about their parents' childhoods. That fascination grows as they advance in age and wisdom and can be satisfied to some degree by looking at a family tree, but how far back does it go? Ultimately, "Where did I come from?" becomes an important question.

Philosophers and theologians talk about "existential neurosis," a kind of psychological stress experienced by a person who neglects to investigate his purpose and the outcome of his inevitable death. "Why am I here?" and "Where am I going?" sum it up well. Viktor Frankl, in his book *Man's Search for Meaning,* says, "The meaning of our existence is not invented by ourselves, but rather detected.Ó Frankl, a Jewish psychologist who suffered in a Nazi concentration camp during WWII, used his experience to develop a psychological therapy called logotherapy. Logotherapy provides a way for a person to find mental health by understanding the meaning in his life. The very process of exploration can lead to greater stability as it relates to our topic, motivation.

There are only two possibilities when it comes to our human existence. Either we came into existence without God, through random events statistically exceeding what knowledgeable human beings regard as being scientifically probable, or we were, in some way, created by God. There are no other options. As responsible human beings, we should each examine the possibility of God's existence.

If you determine that there is more evidence to support the existence of God than His nonexistence, you should find out what His expectations are for you. Gallup polls have determined that 96 percent of Americans believe in God. If we believe God exists, then we probably believe in the possibility of life after death. What kind of an effect does such a belief have on our lives here on earth?

Legacy achievers take their responsibility to seek out the truth very seriously. A failure to do so can leave a feeling of emptiness.

The history of the United States of America is one of the greatest case studies demonstrating what faith can do as it relates to motivation. This wonderful and powerful country was undeniably founded upon the beliefs of men and women with strong faith. Proof of this is everywhere. Not only was this country founded upon such beliefs, but it was founded because of the desire to worship freely.

The Declaration of Independence gives God credit for all things and clearly states that we have a creator who gave us unalienable rights such as life, liberty, and the pursuit of happiness. Our paper money and coins bear the legend, In God We Trust. Our founding fathers based the legal system on the Ten Commandments.

Even mid-twentieth century leaders of our great nation acknowledged God. In 1952, an act of Congress changed the Pledge of Allegiance to include the wording "under God."

Yet today our society has developed an attitude that we should no longer talk openly about God because we might offend some of those around us. We are all affected by this attitude. As a businessperson, I am limited to what I can say in reference to God when working with corporations. With an eye for the necessity of being politically correct, I am careful not to cross the line when I work with companies.

However, as a motivational speaker and trainer, I have a problem: leaving out faith and spirituality as a reason for success is like leaving out the bread when making a sandwich. It's what holds everything together.

It's ironic that every dollar businesses receive bears the words, In God We Trust, yet it's politically incorrect to mention Him out loud. Who are we trying to protect?

I believe in God. Too much proof exists to deny His existence. If I can be shown that I am wrong then I would accept what is true, but at this point I believe He reveals Himself in many ways. The more I study scripture and history, the more I see that He has a plan for each of us. The more I pray, the more I understand His plan for me.

Understanding God's plan for each of us means we need to spin all six of our plates every day. Whether a plate needs a push, a nudge, or just a mental promise to attend to them soon, they all need our regular attention. Remember, on the days we are unable to actually invest into a new stock, call our mother, serve our neighbor, learn more about our vocation, or find a treadmill to exercise on, there is always time for prayer. God planned it this way.

Remember, there is always time for prayer.

Awareness Is the Start

There is more material available on each of the balance points than most of us have time to read. Magazine articles, books, Internet sites, and other resources are right at your fingertips. However, you already possess the most important thing you need to start balancing your life: you are now aware that you must focus on the six balance points of family, financial responsibility, health, social contribution, education and vocation, and faith. This awareness will make an everlasting impact on your life.

As a businessman, I am constantly reminded of the importance of being aware of the balance points. I often give important statistics to the people I work with, statistics necessary for their business to operate effectively. Many times, even without training or motivating a team, I see sales numbers and other vital business measurements improve by as much as 100 percent, simply as a result of clarifying their target. Awareness is essential to improvement and balance.

However, simply being aware of the balance points will not produce change in your life unless you set your awareness in motion. There is no greater time like the present to bring balance into your life.

Defining the Terms: Pursuing Perfection

Let's return to the Formula for Motivation. I refer to the aspect of balance in the formula as "The Pursuit of Life's Perfect Balance." Perhaps this sounds intimidating. Sometimes words lacking finality, such as *pursuit*, or words with great magnitude, such as *perfect*, make you want to give up before you start.

Relax. As soon as you gain a full understanding of the concepts involved, you'll be excited to accept the challenge.

I use the word *pursuing* rather than *achieving* because *achieving* suggests that people can finish a job and then rest on their laurels. But pursuing balance and maintaining motivation require a lifetime of effort.

I don't claim to be perfect—far from it. I use the word *perfect*—whether as an adjective, noun, or verb—as symbolism for a higher level. No human can ever actually be *perfect*, including having perfect balance. However, perfection is a necessary target because it requires continued effort (pursuit). If you shoot for an abstract goal like "pretty good," you'll have difficulty defining it and may feel as though you have already reached it. Thus you may find yourself floundering in life without a clear direction or purpose.

Picture a surfer. You see him on a surfboard gliding along a huge wave and say to yourself, "Wow, that guy is incredible! What perfect balance."

Just as you say, "What perfect balance," the surfer slips off balance a bit, then gets back on balance, then slips off again, then on again. Although, technically, he never actually attains perfect balance, you call it perfect balance because the surfer never falls. It's more accurate to say he *pursues* perfect balance by leaning in different directions in response to the waves he encounters.

It's impossible for the surfer to attain perfect balance because the ocean, with its tides and currents, moves in unpredictable ways. Likewise, sometimes we lean a little left, we lean a little right. But if we don't fall off our surfboard in life, we too are maintaining a state of perfect balance. Just as the ocean is unpredictable, so are the events in our lives. The more the surfer practices balance, the better prepared he is for the unexpected. With a high level of motivation, our chances for success are great. But we must work on maintaining our balance in life all the time.

PURSUING PERFECTION VERSUS BEING A PERFECTIONIST

Let's look at the difference between pursuing *perfection* in balance and being a *perfectionist*. Where is the perfectionist's focus? On the details, whether they are significant or not. Perfectionists often miss deadlines because they allow minutiae to delay the projects in progress. As opposed to the perfectionist, the person pursuing perfection often recalls the old saying, *the devil is in the details*. That saying cuts both ways. Neglect the details and you will never get anywhere. Overanalyze the details and you will suffer the same fate. The Legacy Achiever balances important details with the big picture and the significant things in life.

It may appear either noble or naïve to pursue perfect balance, knowing it can never actually be achieved. But consider the pursuit noble, understanding that you're reaching for the truly big picture in life.

BE NOT AFRAID

A colleague once asked, "Why don't you call your work on the Formula for Motivation *The Pursuit of Great Balance* or *The Pursuit of Really Good Balance*? Perfection sounds so difficult!"

This is true. But as I talked with legacy achievers, I found that they don't pursue great balance or really good balance in life. To them, those adjectives just aren't measurable; they're much too flexible. Can you define "great"? Or "really good"? These definitions are much too relative for our purpose.

By definition, a square is only a square if its sides are perfectly even. But we still call our imperfect drawing attempts "squares". Perfection is measurable very much in the same way you gauge a young child's efforts to copy a square.

You don't just give a child a great square or a good square to copy because it wouldn't really be a square. You give the child a perfect square as an example, a perfect target . However, we know the child will not get the square exactly right. The child makes something resembling a square. As the young child's instructor or guide, you say,

"Hey, good job! Keep working on it." With that, the pursuit of perfection begins. The following year, when you give the child the same square to duplicate, you expect her to do a little better. If she doesn't draw a more precise square, you work with her. It's about improvement and motivating improvement.

Pursuing perfect balance is a process we go through continuously. Every year as the child grows older, she gets closer to that perfect square. Ultimately, with the appropriate tools and not freehand, the child draws a perfect square, and you say, "Now *that's* perfect."

Likewise, we all need to develop our focus on perfect balance. We also need to forgive ourselves and forgive others when we fall short of our objectives.

To pursue something as profound as perfect balance, you need to realize that you are going to make mistakes. If you feel down or low because you don't attain perfect balance, or don't feel in balance one day, you might want to give up on the whole concept. Some of you may concede, "I just can't do it."

This is where forgiveness comes in. Nobody ever attains perfection. That goal, our life's effort, is always a work in progress. It's wise to go through the process saying, "I know nobody actually attains perfection. The objective is to get as close as I can."

Consider people who think they are perfect or say they've attained perfect balance. The admission itself exposes a flaw. Even legacy achievers don't identify themselves as such. When you're in balance, ultimately the square you copy may not be perfect, but you will have found motivation in your continued pursuit.

The mistakes that we make during our pursuit of perfect balance help form our character and lead us closer to that ever-evasive goal of perfection. Our flaws and imperfections shape us into something beautiful. Think of a flower. When you look at a flower, you may say, "This flower is perfect, how beautiful!" But look closer. You'll see flaws and imperfections. But those very flaws and imperfections create a beautiful flower.

FOCUS ON THE DESTINATION

For another way to look at pursuing perfection, consider how a pilot and copilot fly a jetliner.

About 95 percent of the time, jet planes fly slightly off-course. Today, a computerized autopilot constantly corrects these deviations, but before this technology was available, the pilot and copilot handled the errors. They didn't smack each other on the head and say, "Hey, you're off course by a degree. Keep this up and we'll wind up in San Diego instead of Los Angeles."

The pilots' primary focus was on where they were scheduled to go. They didn't pay much attention to being slightly off course at any given moment. They didn't even consider the situation to be a problem; they simply made the necessary corrections as a normal part of the process.

Like a surfer or a pilot, look at the deviations in your journey toward perfect balance as routine and make the necessary course corrections—they are simply part of the process. Make whatever adjustments you need to make today to get on track, knowing that tomorrow life may throw you a curve, and you need to be prepared to make other adjustments, rebalance, and get back on course again.

A Big Lesson from a Little Bit

An American company developed a drill bit as thin as a human hair. At the time, this was considered an amazing technological feat.

The company introduced its amazing drill bit all over the world, and it sent samples to Germany, Russia, and Japan.

The Russians didn't respond, no doubt due to the fall of communism and other more pressing matters.

The Germans were extremely interested. Their response: Send all the information you can. How did you develop this? What are the applications? How could this bit be used in our marketplace?

The Japanese simply mailed the drill bit back *with a hole drilled through it*! They had been quietly developing an even greater, more precise technology.

The point is, no matter how great or perfect we might think we are, there is always room for improvement. We might say to ourselves, "I don't want to put the effort into improving my life. It's fine just the way it is."

But for how long? Without a focus on improvement, we are only capable of handling the same types of challenges that life has already given us. People who want to stretch themselves, train for upcoming and unexpected challenges, maintaining their fitness for life's adventures.

And what about people who have a *my-life-is-fine-just-the-way-it-is* attitude? They're going to have to grow and face life's unexpected challenges anyway. Unfortunately, being forced to grow is generally more painful than choosing to grow.

Inspiring Examples

Authors Jack Canfield and Mark Victor Hansen put together a compilation of stories about well-known people who have overcome difficulties to accomplish great things. Examples such as these are an inspiration for us in our pursuit of life's perfect balance.

The authors told us that after Fred Astaire's first screen test, MGM's testing director wrote, "Can't act, slightly bald, can dance a little." When Astaire became one of Hollywood's greatest stars, he had this memo framed and hung over the fireplace in his palatial Beverly Hills home.

An expert said of Vince Lombardi, "He possesses minimal football knowledge and lacks motivation." Can you believe how far wrong the *expert*'s assessment was? Today, Vince Lombardi is heralded as one of the greatest motivators of modern times, and he amassed one of the greatest records any NFL coach ever achieved.

Louisa May Alcott, author of the classic *Little Women*, was encouraged by her family to find work as a servant or seamstress.

Beethoven handled the violin awkwardly and preferred playing his own compositions to improving his violin technique. His teachers considered him hopeless as a composer.

The vocal coach of the famous opera singer, Enrico Caruso, said he had no voice and could not sing. His parents wanted him to become an engineer.

A newspaper editor fired Walt Disney for lack of ideas.

Thomas Edison's teacher said he was too stupid to learn anything.

Albert Einstein did not speak until he was four years

old and did not read until he was seven. His teachers described him as mentally slow, unsociable, and adrift forever in his foolish dreams. He was refused admittance to the Zurich Polytechnic School.

Henry Ford went broke five times before he finally succeeded as an automotive entrepreneur.

Babe Ruth, considered by many sports historians to be the greatest athlete of all time, is famous for setting a home run record that wasn't approached for many years. Ruth also struck out more than any other batter.

Eighteen publishers turned down Richard Bach's ten-thousand-word story, *Jonathan Livingston Seagull*, before McMillan published it in 1970. By 1975, the book had sold more than seven million copies in the U.S. alone.

When we find ourselves feeling discouraged, it helps to know that others have felt the same way but didn't give up. Their focus and motivation allowed them to continue to pursue greatness in their lives. The same can hold true for us.

> *It helps to know that others have felt the same way but did not give up.*

The pursuit of perfection is a lifetime pursuit that includes failures and often harsh criticism from others. You must be wise enough to forgive your own mistakes, and strong enough to stay on track when you are fairly or unfairly judged by others.

When I was a young man about to begin my first job, my dad's advice was to listen to my critics. He said I would often learn more from them than I would from those who gave me praise.

Beginning the process of living a highly motivated and balanced life is not out of anyone's reach. But to do so, you

MOTIVATION = **Balance** + Influence + (Creativity + Humor) – Runaway Self-Esteem

must focus on your reasons for wanting to balance your life, never on the excuses for not doing so.

People who strive for perfection become more aware of the work they must accomplish in life when they have a lofty and specific target. People who have no specific target can stagnate in life.

In a speech to Parliament on June 8, 1944, Prime Minister Winston Churchill, referring to World War I, said, "I'm sure the mistakes of the time will not be repeated. We shall probably make a whole new set of mistakes." Churchill's statement describes human nature. Of course, his prediction came true.

Forgiving yourself for your mistakes is not the same as compromising your standards. You must not become complacent and accept your mistakes as inevitable. That attitude would amount to quitting before you even get started.

You must always hold yourself to a higher standard. You must learn to recognize the difference between accepting your mistakes, which can be a recipe for failure, and forgiving yourself for them. You must remain motivated and continue your pursuit of life's perfect balance.

What Is Your Role in Life?

In order to help provide meaning to your pursuit of life's perfect balance, you must discover your role in this world. To do this you must examine your God-given talents and gifts.

Here's a thought I've often had. If we could take *The Guinness Book of World Records* and ask every single person on earth to try and break every record in the book, I believe it would only be a matter of days before we would be rewriting most of the records.

Think about our planet's six billion inhabitants. Among this vast number of people, how many individuals who have never put on track shoes could be world-class sprinters?

How many people who have never put on track shoes could be faster than the greatest Olympic athletes of our day?

How many people could write beautiful poetry if they ever picked up a pen for that purpose?

How many people have the natural talent to play musical instruments but have never tried to develop their talent?

Contemplating your direction in life can be exciting to think about. We all need to find our talents and our purpose. The pursuit of perfection guides us toward this discovery.

The almost overused example of Roger Banister still resonates today with people in both business and athletics. On May 6, 1954, Banister ran the first sub-four-minute mile. He ran the mile in three minutes and fifty-nine seconds, thus ending the athletic world's long-running quest to break the four-minute mile.

Today, high school students run sub-four-minute miles regularly and not because Nike came out with a better shoe. It's because high school students now believe they can accomplish the same feat.

Banister's role in life goes well beyond breaking a track record. His dramatic accomplishment shapes the minds of many people who face today's challenges.

It's doubtful whether Banister could have imagined what an enormous impact his story would still be having on the world of athletics and business decades after the event. You may be equally unaware of the effect your results and achievements have on others.

Even if your "Roger Banister experience" is that you're the only one in your office who can manage voice-mail, e-mail, and irritating customers all at one time without losing your cool, your example still may inspire others to become their best self. By your example they will see that it's possible to break the four-minute mile of self-control in the work place.

Take It to the Next Level

On a more serious note, I once had the pleasure of meeting U.S. Airforce Colonel Edward L. Hubbard (Retired). His story really impressed me.

Colonel Hubbard talked about how he was ordered to get up before dawn one day to fly a mission over enemy territory. He said, "You always know it's going to be a bad day when it's still dark when you get up."

During a speech, he asked his audience, "How many of you have had a bad day before?" Everyone raised a hand. "Let me see if I can put a bad day into perspective," he continued.

As he was flying over enemy territory, Hubbard's plane was hit. He ejected from his aircraft while it was flying at about six hundred miles an hour. Hubbard described what it was like to hit the air at that speed. He said it was like hitting a brick wall. The impact was so great, he was blinded.

The colonel fell through the dark sky, blind and painfully aware that he was being shot at from the ground. He did what anyone would do. He reached up to feel his face to learn the extent of the injury and gratefully realized that he wasn't blind. His helmet had spun around on his head and covered his face.

When he turned the helmet around, he saw a terrifying sight—enemy fire was coming right at him. He landed without being hit, but he was immediately captured and spent many years as a prisoner of war.

Some things he accomplished to keep himself alive in prison were absolutely amazing. Colonel Hubbard knew that to survive in prison he needed to keep physically and mentally sharp.

A COMPETITION

A Navy friend just a couple of cells away assisted his physical survival. The Navy man challenged him to a push-ups contest. He communicated to Hubbard, "Let's see how many we can do."

Hubbard took up the challenge. He got down on the floor and performed 100 push-ups. But his Navy friend did 150 and said, "I win."

Hubbard replied, "Okay, let's do it again. Only next time, you go first." Hubbard figured this time he'd know what his competition was, and then he could beat him.

After a few weeks of preparation, the contest commenced. The Navy friend powered 200 push-ups. So Hubbard followed with 220 push-ups, winning the contest. For the next encounter, the Naval pilot asked the Colonel to go first. They repeated the whole process. This time, Colonel Hubbard performed 300 consecutive push-ups. His Navy friend did 600 push-ups in a row.

Wisely, Colonel Hubbard said, "I don't want to do this contest anymore. Let's do sit-ups."

So, they had a sit-ups contest, and the Colonel's friend completed 2,000 sit-ups in row. Now, Colonel Hubbard had never done more than 115 sit-ups, the number required for his Air Force officer fitness test. But he ended up doing 2,700 consecutive sit-ups to win the contest.

Keep in mind, these feats were accomplished on a prison diet that was often as low as three hundred calories a day. A normal diet would provide about two thousand calories.

When you think you don't have enough energy to accomplish your goal, remember that you can take it to the next level.

Sometimes when you think you're tapped out physically and don't have enough energy to accomplish your goal, remember that you can—as these men did—take it to the next level. You are capable of taking all your quests to levels that seem out of reach at this moment.

MIND GAMES

To maintain mental sharpness during his years of captivity, Colonel Hubbard conducted mental feats as impressive as his physical achievements. He accomplished these amazing mental acts in the stressful setting of a prison camp, while witnessing other patriots being beaten by guards. Prisoners were not allowed to speak to each other. Talking meant a beating or even death.

One way the prisoners communicated was with a tap code, a method the military taught them. Picture a square grid containing twenty-five boxes, five boxes across by five boxes down. Each box contains a letter of the alphabet starting with a in the upper-left corner. (The letter k was eliminated because c could be substituted for it.)

To communicate using tap code, prisoners would tap the number of boxes a letter is across and down. For example, tap three times for the letter c, the third box to the right in the top row.

Imagine tapping out just one word. To speed the tedious process a little, the prisoners developed codes for certain words. But to communicate, they still had to tap everything—but one thing they had plenty of was time.

Colonel Hubbard and other prisoners who wanted to stay mentally fit were determined to keep on learning while in prison. Just envision the psychological difficulties coming from sitting in a prison camp for years, unable to even speak to another person.

So they tapped to each other and asked, "What do you know that I don't know? What do I know that you don't know? Let's share all we know." Tap. Tap. Tap.

One man spoke Spanish. So Colonel Hubbard decided to learn Spanish in tap code. He excelled in the language. Tap. Tap. Tap.

When released years later, the Colonel visited a university near his home and asked the Spanish professor if he could take the final exam. Hubbard passed the final although he had never spoken the language before he took the test.

I recommend the Colonel Hubbard's book *Escape from*

the Box: The Wonder of Human Potential. We can all use these stories of courage and triumph as a source of strength when we feel ourselves losing balance or motivation.

An Incremental Process

Pursuing life's perfect balance is about incremental improvement. The pursuit is also about forgiveness. You need to forgive your mistakes along the way because mistakes are part of the process. Focus on making fewer and fewer mistakes as you proceed on your journey. As you pay attention to all six of life's balance points, you will maintain your motivation to lead a good life. Like the legacy achievers, you must focus on becoming a more effective person as time goes on.

Motivation, Balance, and Time Management

The Balancing Act—Stacking Plates

One of the most important skills that legacy achievers master is time management. Legacy achievers are not machines who are programmed to be effective in time management and life balance. They know that it takes time to spin each of the balance plates. That is why they use a method called *stacking*. They pile one plate on top of another—managing more than one balance point at a time—whenever possible. I have joked in seminars that the most illustrative example of stacking plates is golfing in a charity outing—without a cart, in a foursome that includes your financial advisor, wife, and mentor—and praying before each swing.

That would cover each of the six balance points. Obviously, this would be impossible to pull off even one time, let alone daily. But the point is, stacking plates is an effective way to save time and focus on what is important. Whatever the stacking combination, the outcome is usually positive. In fact, studies have shown that people who use the stacking approach to balance their lives, instead of separating responsibilities, are able to sustain a higher level of motivation. People who integrate the balance points by involving family in their work objectives, health goals, spiritual growth, and other balance points will sustain and even grow in motivation. Each balance point acts as mortar for the other. (Kristin Byron, 2005)

Many people exercise with their loved ones or pray while they jog.

Some people believe the concept of balancing (and stacking) their life sounds great, but they feel ill-equipped to make changes or put the concepts into action. I developed a patented time management system to aid them in their efforts. If you want to get your life in order, you must go beyond the *idea* of balance and enter into the *action* of balance. This action is made possible by maintaining the proper focus, establishing habits, getting and staying organized, and managing tasks. The time management system I developed is called the **Balander**™. The name is derived from blending the words *balance* and *calendar*—it is literally a *balance calendar*. It's designed to support the person using the formula for motivation in the previously mentioned areas of success, especially: 1) maintaining proper focus and establishing healthy habits, and 2) managing tasks and responsibilities.

Maintaining Proper Focus and Establishing Healthy Habits

Talk to anyone who has pushed himself to the brink of exhaustion, and he'll tell you that a huge remedy for his fatigue was prioritizing his responsibilities. Most people make big plans at the beginning of each year: lose twenty-five pounds, learn a foreign language, play more with the children, listen to our spouse's concerns, save for retirement, and so on. But we find ourselves giving up by February because our efforts bore no fruit in January. This happens because we failed to see our long-term plans in our daily calendar.

Maintaining a proper focus means keeping the plates spinning every day. Human beings can spin six plates, but there is not a lot of room for error. You need to form the habit of spinning each plate daily if you want to gain motivation and, equally important, if you want to keep it. The Balander™ is a tool that can empower you to keep your plates spinning each day. You need to give attention, in your planner, to each of the six plates every day. You must determine how you will fulfill your responsibilities for each one. If you find yourself at a loss for ideas on how to affect any given plate, it's probably a sign of atrophy in that area of your life. Dig down deep and find a way, even if it is very basic. Don't move from one day to the next without committing at least some time to each plate. It doesn't need to be a lot of time. Some people make the mistake of thinking that they need to divide time for the six plates equally into each twenty-four hours. Some days, spending just ten to thirty minutes on some of the plates is enough. Other days the same plates may require hours.

You may have heard the well-known story of the college professor who had a big glass jar with large rocks stacked in it up to the brim. He asked his students whether the jar was full, and they replied that it was. He then filled in the gaps with small stones and repeated his question. The students caught on and said that there really was room remaining in the jar. To support their observation, the professor filled in the remaining space with water. He then asked, "What's the lesson as it relates to time management?" The students collectively answered, "You can always fit more in." In response, the professor said, "You've missed the point. The lesson is this: If you want to get the big rocks in, they must go in first. In other words, the important things in life must be handled first."

It's difficult to argue with that thinking, and considering the emphasis I put on the spinning plates, you probably assume I'd agree. Well, in theory I do agree, but in application I disagree.

Here's why. In the many years that I've helped people overcome their time management challenges, more often than not I've seen that the little things drive people to irrational behavior. In the short term, it is not the big issues that cause a person to mismanage their time. Even the most competent professional has admitted that what gets her unraveled isn't her marriage or her mortgage—it's the fact that she's two thousand miles over on her oil change, behind on thank-you notes, living with three loads of laundry stacked up on the kitchen table, and weeks overdue on getting her hair colored.

We all have had equivalent *minor* things send us into a tizzy. So I recommend scheduling the little things in your daily plan first—not because they are more important, but because they are generally the justification we provide for not doing what *is* important . Once the little things are in the daily calendar, it's much easier to focus on what is truly important. That may sound like a backward, defeatist approach, but I would much rather hear you complain that I provide backward-sounding advice that works than brilliant advice that fails! And my advice does work. So . . . put the little rocks in first. Then when you get to the big rocks, you will be free to appreciate and enjoy them— you won't be spending precious time thinking about getting your oil changed.

Time once reported on a related study. In the study, people were asked what the greatest source of happiness was in their lives. The respondents who were parents said that their children were the greatest source of happiness. But when the same people were asked a more specific question, which focused on their greatest source of happiness for the *current* day, children barely showed up on the radar. In fact, the top items on the list were all superficial activities such as watching TV.

The survey s illustrates the idea that the big issues do not always drive our behavior. Ironically, what actually *drives* most people's behavior on a daily basis are the very things that impede their greatest satisfactions in life. To alter the imagery the professor used, it could be said that if you don't drain the water and sand from the pool of daily life first, they'll begin to erode the big rocks, those things that matter most to us.

If we master the minor issues, we'll naturally be better at mastering the major ones.

Managing Tasks and Responsibilities

The methods with which you spin your plates and carry out minor tasks play a big role in determining your personal success. I developed the Balander™ because the planners and electronic programs that existed on the market did not (and still don't) offer a complete method for integrating your entire life into a simple solution. Either the planners were too complicated, accommodating a person who lives a complex life, or they were incomplete. I set out to design a practical planner that someone could learn to use in fifteen minutes, in contrast to the day-long seminars that most others required. I wanted this planner to be a powerful tool that applies to the most complex professional schedule and is also practical for managing the kids' games and a household.

Obviously, I hope you'll think about my own method, but whatever approach you take, remember that we all have two prominent needs in order to keep our plates spinning. We need:

1. The ability to see our day, month, and year all at in one view
2. A *tomorrow* to do list

These two points will help take our motivation to the next level.

The Full View

If you use a daily planner or a PDA, you know how frustrating it can be to see only the current day or the current month without any daily details. If someone requests your presence next Thursday you flip pages or scroll until it shows up. You must then flip or scroll to the prior day and the following day to see what Thursday butts up against. The feeling is like driving in fog.

Some others of you own a monthly planner that does let you see the entire month in front of you, but it lacks planning and writing space for any given day. It is probably filled with arrows and other scribbling in the margins.

The Balander™ allows you to see your day, month, and year all in one glance. Thus preventing you from over-booking or from feeling unsure of what tomorrow will bring. In addition, that same view includes a full page for note taking, a daily page that begins at 5:00 A.M. and ends at 11:00 P.M., plus a master task list called the "Tomorrow To Do List."

Tomorrow To Do List

Ironically it is not a person's irresponsibility that prevents him from managing tasks. It is his untamed sense of responsibility. For example, you have your entire day planned out but something important comes up. Your sense of responsibility tells you that you must address the

MOTIVATION = **Balance** + Influence + (Creativity + Humor) – Runaway Self-Esteem

issue immediately. You remember many fancy, great-sounding, yet misapplied positive quotes like "Carpe diem" ("seize the day" in Latin), "There's no time like the present" or "If it is to be it is up to me"! These quotes motivate you to move into action on the immediate albeit unplanned task, thus pushing you behind on your established plan. The result is that you appear unorganized or irresponsible, neither of which are true. Instead, you are lacking restraint on your sense of responsibility.

A Tomorrow To Do List will prevent you from opening up your e-mail account to send an important message only to be derailed by an incoming message that needs your attention. The unexpected e-mail leads to a phone call with a business partner who reminds you that you need to fill out a report for the upcoming staff meeting. Mention of that report reminds you that you should really get going on your expense reports. Oh yeah, and how are you going to find the receipts you misplaced on your last trip? Two hours later (or worse, the entire day goes by), and you never even sent the original e-mail you had intended to send.

Here is the best way to stay on top of your tasks and therefore remain motivated to get through your day in a positive manner.

1. Begin each day with your Tomorrow To Do List (TTDL) at hand. When something that was not a part of your original plan comes up, write it on your TTDL. The act of cataloging it reduces stress and allows you to stay focused on your current plan.

2. As you go throughout your day, when things come up add them to your list.

3. At the end of the day, add anything else that you need to accomplish the next day.

DON'T STOP THERE. Now that you have a list to plan from, you have to keeping working the drill. This is where many time management errors are made, leaving the user of the list flailing throughout the day. So here is the continuation:

4. One of the main reasons why people who use to do lists fail to complete them is because they do not apply a specific time to each of the tasks. Anecdotally, you are five time more likely to accomplish your tasks if you have a specific time attached to each one. (If you have a Balander™, simply fold the TTDL over and you will see that it matches up with the next day's hourly agenda. The times are purposely on the right side of the page so you can write in your tasks in a specific time slot)

5. Now look at the items you have entered for your day. You probably have a mix of pebbles, sand, water, and big rocks. Look at the list of six plates and determine which ones are missing. Find a place to add them. Don't stop until you have included each one of them.

MOTIVATION = **Balance** + Influence + (Creativity + Humor) – Runaway Self-Esteem

Some of you may have been trained to use a "floating to do list." The concept is that if you have items that you need to do but you don't know when you will be able to do them, you can put them on this master list. This is a great mechanisms for instilling a low level of motivation. If you are like 99.9% of the people in the world, this list could easily be called the "stuff I will never do but I will look at to feel guilty list." Scrap the idea and replace it with the following: If you know you can't do something tomorrow then don't write it on your TTDL. Instead, put it on a TTDL that is realistic. Maybe you will not get to it until next Thursday. If that is the case, put it on next Wednesday's TTDL. The fact that it is on Wednesday's list is invaluable. Many victims of "oops I forgot" suffered their fate because they placed an item on a to do list for a day in the future and never looked at it until they woke up that day. The lack of a heads-up can prevent them from keeping the commitment. Using the TTDL for future planning is great to provide an advanced reminder of what is to come.

Part Two

Tactical Components

*Try not to become a man of success but
rather try to become a man of value.*

—Albert Einstein

Integrity-Based Influence

People are the most unpredictable variable affecting motivation in our daily lives. Some of the people we interact with "get in the way" of our plans for success, and others help us along. The way in which you manage your relationships will either fuel or squelch your level of motivation.

The way in which you exercise your influence is a major factor in the health of your relationships, and no matter what your place is in life you have some influence over other people. Even the lowest person on the ladder has people in his life who are influenced by his actions, words, or emotions. This can be witnessed by small children who, despite their diminutive size and lack of authority, use their influence to "force" their parents to respond to their every whim. Many weak parents actually say, "But he forced me to."

When adults use their power, whether authoritative or relational, to manipulate others they will eventually self-destruct because people are not meant to be a means to an end; they are an end in and of themselves.

When one person tries to get something out of another strictly to attain a goal or to reach an objective, they run the risk of treating the other party as an *object* rather than a *subject*. No doubt, there are sad examples of this all over the world. One of the most obvious is the way in which many men use women as an object for their own personal physical gratification. That is not to say women can't be guilty of the same. To the manipulator, the outcome seems like no big deal, but the person who was used can be hurt by the experience.

Robert Greene, the very popular author of books such as the *48 Laws of Power* and the *Conscious Art of Seduction,* has made a living teaching people to treat others as objects. The cover of the *Art of Seduction* actually tells the potential reader that they will learn how to target a "victim" in order to use their weaknesses against them. That may sound so over the top that you trivialize the impact of such a book. Sadly, all it takes is a few conversations with his many disciples to see that his perspective and strategies are embraced by many.

Integrity-based influence is about getting, building, and maintaining motivation through healthy relationships. That means treating other people as subjects not objects.

To illustrate the point, think about the ways in which we call a ball an object. You can kick it, pop it, throw it, and manipulate it in any way you want. But a subject, like mathematics or history, can't be manipulated. A subject can only be discovered, explored, and investigated. When you get to "know" a subject, you soon gain respect for it. You see a subject's value. Once you know the subject's value you may use it to advance a particular cause, but that use of a subject does not dominate your relationship with it because the subject remains larger than the cause.

Likewise, when you get to know someone as a person, you will see them as a subject, with the inherent value of their personhood. You may want to learn more about them, and if there is a good match you may want that person to help you advance a cause, but only if there is something to be gained for that person as well as for you and your cause. Sometimes this is a brief interaction, but the outcome is the same. The breakfast waitress goes from being a machine who distributes hot coffee to a woman who is trying to provide for her children. The "hot girl" at the beach becomes someone's daughter and future wife.

In other words the person who manipulates people as objects for their own gain uses those people as tools, but a legacy achiever acts as a partner with others for the benefit of both parties.

Reflecting on the many years I've spent researching influence, the primary thing ringing in my head is the importance of integrity. Besides the previously stated books, numerous other books have been written on how to influence others, most of them based on a less overt but nonthe-less disappointing popular philosophy about influence.

MOTIVATION = Balance + **Influence** + (Creativity + Humor) – Runaway Self-Esteem

This philosophy essentially teaches people to do, speak, or act in any way possible to advance their cause, with little or no mention of the importance of integrity.

Readers are told they'll find techniques in these popular books to convince people to do what they want, without considering anyone's feelings, well-being, or rights except their own. Not surprisingly, since the authors urge disregard for the legitimate needs of others, few of the techniques can deliver on the books' promises. However, this is beside the point.

Due to my own immaturity, early in my career when I found some techniques that did work, I used them. I regret doing so. That being said, the lessons I learned from my mistakes are invaluable. Now I can see the greater problem: in those days I always justified my actions. My conscience was in constant turmoil, but my results as a businessperson were incredible. Sales boomed.

When confronted by my conscience, I rationalized that I was simply implementing what I had learned from my studies. Besides, I wasn't doing anything that the general population would have considered wrong. In fact, most people would have considered using such techniques prudent. As a result, I became and remained a master of a successful influencing technique until I could no longer handle the pain in my heart.

A new challenge faced me. If I abandoned the self-centered techniques that worked so well for me, could I still get solid sales results? Could I follow my conscience and still be successful? I was in a crisis. I could not continue as I was. My motivation was deteriorating because I was not being true to my conscience.

I took a leap of faith and began to monitor everything I said from the perspective of the other person in the conversation. After what I considered a brief correctional period, my results were even greater than they had been before.

When you aren't true to your conscience, your motivation deteriorates.

Focusing on the other person did not mean excluding all the information and techniques I'd been taught about influence. Although most of that information lacked integrity, not all of it did. Not using anything I had learned would be throwing the baby out with the bath water. The difference was that I not only incorporated integrity into how I influenced others, I put it first.

I am thankful that I learned this lesson prior to assuming a substantial leadership role. Learning the same lesson while having a lot of people reporting to me would have caused me deeper regret.

The negative effects of *technique-driven influence tactics* can be seen most clearly in sales management. Sales managers often teach their salespeople a technique called a "tie down." An example of a tie down would be to look at someone and nod your head up and down in the yes motion as you deliver a loaded question such as, "So you would like to buy it, right?" Admittedly, such head nodding is a natural unconscious tendency, but when it is done to consciously manipulate others, it lacks integrity. The objective is to get the customer so wrapped up in your body language and voice inflection that they essentially forget their own opinion and do as you say.

As if this isn't bad enough, sales managers often use the same technique directly on the salespeople they're

MOTIVATION = Balance + **Influence** + (Creativity + Humor) – Runaway Self-Esteem

managing. They will look directly at the sales reps, with their head nodding vigorously up and down, and say, "So you will get the samples ready for me by nine o'clock, *right*?"

If the reps are paying attention, they will know they are being manipulated in the same disrespectful manner that they were taught to treat their own customers. Here's the good news: many people in the world are influential without being manipulative.

The objective of this chapter is to share with you how influence fits into the life of a legacy achiever. As I mentioned earlier, my motivation to continue to work hard deteriorated when I did not follow my conscience. I was using influence tactically, but without integrity. While today's society wouldn't call anything I did unethical, I knew in my heart that something wasn't right. One's ethics should not be measured by society's deteriorated state, but by the standard of right and wrong.

In business we are often faced with ethical decisions. An attorney advised me on a way to keep a foreign businessperson in the country after her work visa expired. He explained how to fill out the paperwork to satisfy the government.

"We'll never have to honor the letter as long as the government doesn't find out," the attorney added.

"That would lack integrity," I said.

"People do this all the time," he responded.

Unfortunately this attitude is all too common today. The attorney was using the absence of other people's integrity and society's lamentable state to justify his own lack of integrity. Of course we honored the terms of the letter.

By Itself, Influence Is Not Enough

Rather than placing our focus on influence alone, I urge *integrity-based influence* (IBI) as the most powerful tactical component of motivation.

Integrity-based influence is necessary in living a motivated life for many reasons. Time and time again, I meet with people who are unhappy in their jobs because their employers ask them to take actions that offend their ethics or morals. For example, salespeople are often trained to provide false information to secure a sale. Middle managers are told to lie to employees to cover up their superior's unethical practices.

Trainers or managers who lack integrity teach their salespeople to do the same—without admitting what they are doing. Rather, they call their unprincipled advice a *sales technique* and persist with this disguise even though everyone knows what they are doing.

When top executives ask a middle manager to lie, they usually buddy up to the manager with a talk about future opportunities. Or they let the manager in on a secret so he feels important. This way, the manager has a greater incentive to lie.

When managers are pressured to lie to or manipulate others, they must make a decision. Usually they have only two options: lower their moral standards in order to fit in, or quit. This major cause of employee turnover in corporations is especially damaging to the firms involved because it usually drives away their best and brightest managers.

Sometimes there's a third option—which often turns out to be only a temporary solution. The manager can refuse to lie and hang on in hopes that the corporate culture will change in time to save their jobs. It rarely happens that way, and hanging on may diminish their prospects or even incur open hostility from upper management. If the middle manager elects to stay, no matter which option he chooses after having been pressed to lie, his motivation deteriorates.

Succumbing to pressures that compromise your integrity is detrimental, but choosing to do so on our own is truly destructive. If you do this, you will lose your perpetual motivation either through suffering from a guilty conscience or from eventual being exposed as untrustworthy.

Exercising your influence can help you guard your time and emotions against outside factors that are inconsistent with living in balance. In life you are constantly pulled in many directions. If you lack the ability to effectively influence others, you can lose control of your life. However, using integrity-based influence will help you on your way to experiencing perpetual motivation.

Seven Identifiable Traits of People Practicing Integrity-Based Influence

Seven identifiable traits are consistently present in the behavior of people who use integrity-based influence, many of whom become legacy achievers. These traits are not techniques. In other words, we are not going to focus on what legacy achievers do to people in order to influence them. Instead we'll zero in on the characteristics from which legacy achievers derive their ability to influence others.

TRAIT #1: KEEP YOUR EMOTIONS ON A LEASH

Although I rarely watch daytime television talk shows, curiosity got the best of me when I passed by a television while leaving the gym one day. I saw a woman relate a traumatic experience she'd had on a Sunday. The lady concluded with, " . . . and so from then on Sundays, have become my depression days," thus dooming herself to being unhappy one-seventh of the rest of her life.

A traumatic event can anchor itself to certain circumstances, in this case Sundays, and cause us to recall unwanted emotions when similar circumstances arise—this is understandable. Nevertheless, if we want to live a motivated life, we must learn to control our emotions and not respond uncontrollably to particular triggers.

Before you can influence others in positive ways, you need to be able to influence yourself positively. If you allow yourself to perpetuate the emotions generated by the negative events of your life, you condemn yourself to fighting a never-ending battle with self-inflicted demotivation.

The talk show guest, behaving irrationally, transferred an extreme aversion to a day of the week. Even though most people commonly behave more rationally than that, many endlessly dwell on past mistakes and unfortunate experiences. It's a habit, and like all habits, it can be broken.

It's difficult to influence others if we can't control our own emotions, and appear weak or unstable. In addition, our uncontrolled emotions can cloud our ability to make good decisions.

When our emotions flare up, identifying where they came from and what they are trying to make us do is vital. For example, consider the natural defense mechanism

MOTIVATION = Balance + **Influence** + (Creativity + Humor) – Runaway Self-Esteem

called *fight or flight*. This instinct, triggered by fear, is built into every human being. If we are in a life-threatening situation and fail to convert our fear into action, we will probably die. Generally the source of the fear is obvious, but if not, we must identify it. Then we must make a decision to either separate ourselves from the danger or face and fight it.

Typically, our emotions ignite in situations that involve fear, depression, guilt, anxiety, or some other negative feeling. Our first step in dealing with this kind of situation should be to analyze where the negative emotion comes from, and then decide whether we can or should gather more information before choosing flight or fight.

Sometimes there'll be no time for such niceties, but if the situation is a recurring one, we will have ample opportunity to study the problem and determine our best course of action. However, a decision such as submitting to making Sundays an automatic day of depression is tantamount to being immobilized, with no chance to attain a fully motivated life .

As long as a person does not suffer from a physiological problem, it's safe to say they could do what many legacy achievers do in this type of situation. Legacy achievers keep their emotions on a leash. They control their emotions rather than letting their emotions control them. In other words, they don't let their emotions run free.

Legacy achievers control their emotions rather than letting their emotions control them.

Emotions can be like a dog that chases a car until it sees a bus, then chases the bus until it sees a bike, and so on until eventually the dog can't find its way back home. We must allow ourselves to express our emotions in appropriate ways, but not to become lost in them.

Whenever possible, legacy achievers preplan their emotional strategies. For example, a legacy achiever in the sales profession is aware of the daily and unavoidable objections to be faced; she will wisely consider an appropriate emotional response to these rejections. One legacy achiever I know has a sixty-second rule. He allows himself sixty seconds to gain control of his emotions when things don't go well selling. This strategy turns mastering his emotions into a game. In his mind, he scores a point for every second short of a minute that it takes to overcome his emotions.

It is strategic to contemplate, though not to dwell on, inevitable situations that will stir our emotions. When facing an unpleasant inevitability, people often say, "I don't even want to think about it!" Such avoidance will only keep us unprepared emotionally. Contemplating and preplanning emotional reactions can help us deal with situations when they arise.

This does not mean we can contemplate and prepare for all the potential tragedies in life. Experiencing the emotional trauma of what it would be like to lose all our family members in a sudden accident is not an accurate interpretation of this trait. On the other hand, if a close friend or relative has a terminal condition, it's wise to prepare yourself for their death.

On a less serious but still stressful topic, if your company is downsizing and you know you may be next, don't ignore the probability. Face it. Prepare yourself to accept the situation if you become a casualty of the change. Your preparation should include developing a plan to move past the misfortune, hopefully turning it into your good fortune.

When all is said and done, legacy achievers handle their emotions in a similar way to what is asked for in the Serenity Prayer:

> God grant me the serenity to accept the things I cannot change, the courage to change the things I can, *and the wisdom to know the difference.*

TRAIT #2: USE HARMONY AND CONVICTION IN VERBAL COMMUNICATION

"Mean what you say and say what you mean" is a cliché summary of this second integrity-based influencing trait. Legacy achievers accomplish this by speaking in harmony with what they stand for, and they do so with conviction.

A study published by Dr. Albert Meridian at Berkeley shows that verbal communication contains three components. These components are: the *word choices* we make, the *voice qualities* we use, and our *physiology*.

His study found that the words we use represent only 7 percent of our influence on others. Our *voice quality*—made up of our tone, tempo, and volume—represents 38 percent of our influence. Finally our *physiology*, or body language, makes up the balance and majority of our influence by accounting for 55 percent of it.

This information could very easily lead a person down the wrong path of influence. Non-integrity-based influential people choose to amplify their manipulative skills by practicing techniques that make effective use of Dr. Meridian's findings. I've seen this happen. It results in transparent communicators limited to influencing people who are weaker than themselves.

Instead, a legacy achiever or other integrity-based influential person uses this information to determine whether he or she may be accidentally sending the wrong messages by presenting unintentional inconsistencies in his or her delivery. This is not a painless thing to do. It may require us to recognize a fault of which we were previously unaware. With the permission of everyone involved, videotaping or audiotaping some of the conversations we have is an excellent way to identify communication inconsistencies so we can eliminate them.

I often have my own speeches videotaped to see what message the audience received in comparison to the message I intended to deliver. It can be a very humbling experience to be in your own audience, but today's technology can help make us aware of our current communication skill level, whatever it might be.

The importance of harmony in our verbal communication skills is illustrated by what happens when we lack harmony. We strike harmony in verbal communication by sending the same message with our word choices, voice quality, and body language. These must also be in agreement with our convictions. If any one of these elements are lacking, the perceived result can range from humor to sarcasm or even rudeness.

Strive to send the same message with your word choices, voice quality, and body language.

If I said the kind words "You look nice" in a harsh voice with a snarl on my face, what message would you perceive?

You might conclude that I think you look stupid. You may think I feel you look nice but am too embarrassed to say it comfortably. You may think I meant what I said, but it came out funny because I was in the middle of a yawn. You may think I'm being rude.

In other words, what should have been a simple communication was hopelessly confused. Whatever I really meant probably didn't get through to you.

When we lack congruency in our message, we leave the recipient guessing at our meaning, which leads to insecurity. This is why legacy achievers are cautious about using sarcasm. People want to know where they stand with one another; sarcasm does not allow for that.

Conviction is also very important; it tends to clarify messages that might otherwise be misinterpreted. Conviction eliminates the need for excess words.

You're an employer. One of your employees asks, "Do you have confidence in me as an employee?" You respond by avoiding eye contact and softly saying, "You're a great employee, and I really appreciate you."

What will he think? Probably he'll doubt that you meant what you said. He may go away far more worried than he was before he asked the question.

On the other hand, if you look him directly in the eyes and firmly say, "Yes," with a strong nod of conviction, he will rest assured that said he understands your response. One word spoken with conviction can be far more effective than an entire speech without it. Of course, an integrity-based influential person would only say yes if he or she really meant it. Remember, this is not about technique; it's about disclosing your true feelings to another person.

TRAIT #3: ANTICIPATE COMMUNICATION
CHALLENGES AND OPPORTUNITIES

Henry Nodland was an interesting fellow. He dressed like a lumberjack and drove a Cadillac. During the 1940s he served as the mayor in a small town in Minnesota. One day this self-made millionaire was driving through a neighboring town when he was pulled over for speeding and was fined fifty dollars. Before he drove on, Henry asked the officer whether he would be in the same area checking traffic later in the day.

"I will," the policeman said.

"Here's another fifty dollars," Henry said. "I'll be coming back!"

When people focus on integrity-based influence, they develop the art of anticipation. While I might question Henry's approach in this day and age, he certainly does illustrate three rules for effective anticipation. First, know where you plan to go. Second, be on the lookout for obstacles. Third, be willing to pay the price for your choices.

Legacy achievers keep these three rules in mind regarding all six balance points. Now let's focus on how the three rules of anticipation affect influence.

Know Where You Plan to Go

Henry asked whether or not the police officer was going to be on the street in a few hours because he knew he'd be driving back through town—over the speed limit. If Henry hadn't planned his day prior to encountering the man in blue, he wouldn't have known to ask the question.

This sounds like a basic concept, and it may be in much of your life. We plan strategies for vacations, meals, parties, and more, But do we plan our communications? During verbal communication with others, we are often caught off guard and become annoyed when we don't have any idea where we're going in our conversation. We may not have the luxury of preparing our objectives for all our communications, but we should be aware of what they are when things really count.

Be on the Lookout for Obstacles

One day upon arriving home from work, my wife, Lisa, greeted me with a concern. Our daughter, Nicole, who was in kindergarten at the time, was concerned about her older brother, Kevin, who attended the same school in the first grade. Nicole told Lisa that some older kids had been tackling Kevin during the week at recess, and it looked like it might be hurting him. Lisa waited for me to arrive home before talking too much about the issue with Kevin. I guess she was thinking I may have had a similar playground experience as a boy and would know whether or not to brush off any concern. She said the only thing she had asked Kevin was whether or not he liked the older kids treating him this way. He told her *he did not like it.*

I was not sure what to think. I didn't like the idea of my son being bullied at school, but I wasn't sure what to say to him. Being a second-degree black belt student, I must admit that for a split second I considered giving him a crash course on self-defense. Then I thought, maybe it would build his character to let him deal with it himself. Then I thought, maybe the best solution would be to talk to a teacher or a parent of one of the older kids. I really didn't know what I should do. But I did know I needed more information.

So I asked him, "Kevin, is there anything you want to tell me about recess today?"

He replied, "No, not really, Dad."

Thinking he might just be afraid to speak out against the other kids, I thought I would prompt him. "Were some older kids tackling you at school today?"

In a quick one-word reply, he said, "Yes."

"Are they playing with you, or is this something you don't like them doing?"

"I don't like it," he responded reluctantly.

It hurt me as a parent to know that my son was being picked on. I had never faced that at school. I felt sorry for him and realized that I needed to give this some thought. But before we ended the conversation, I needed to find out one more thing.

"Kevin, how old were these boys?"

"Dad, they weren't boys!"

I couldn't believe my ears. They weren't boys. "Good grief," I thought, "my son is being bullied by girls! What psychological problems might follow from this in the future?"

Before I could finish my thought, I heard Lisa ask, in a way that only she could have put it, "Kevin, were these girls lovin' ya up or were they beatin' ya up?"

"Loving me up. I don't want to talk about it!"

Now that was the first thing he said in this whole conversation that really made sense to me!

Although this is an example of being caught off guard in a silly conversation, it's a good reminder of how obstacles can impede our communication. We will benefit by anticipating as many potential outcomes as possible to the important conversations we have each day.

In the situation with Kevin, I wasn't able to select a most appropriate action because my preconceptions didn't consider what had actually happened. Thankfully in this case, my best option was to laugh. But that's not always the case.

We benefit by anticipating potential outcomes to the important conversations we have each day.

Attorneys spend weeks preparing for court by role-playing the potential outcomes of cross-examining a witness during a trial. All this, just to prepare for what might be a five-minute conversation. But think of what's at stake; lack of preparation might send an innocent person to prison or let a guilty person walk free. Most of us do not have to deal with outcomes of that magnitude in our daily conversations; still, we must be prepared for the unexpected in a conversation to effectively influence others.

Be Prepared to Pay the Price

Back in Minnesota, Henry knew where he wanted to go, and he identified an obstacle that could slow him down. Faced with this reality, Henry decided to pay the price ahead in order to save time. Integrity-based influential people are also prepared in advance to pay the price for their choices. In this case, we are talking about the price of ridicule or rejection when taking a position or stance we feel is important.

Other people will not always see eye to eye with us. Legacy achievers have learned to meet these occasions with integrity. At one time or another, we have all been in a situation where our position was unpopular. In the face of this dilemma, the pressure to compromise one's beliefs and follow the crowd is strong. If you allow this to happen, you lose our integrity, weaken your ability to influence others, and lose your ability to maintain a high level of motivation.

Am I urging you to adopt an adamantly closed mind, allow no compromise, and maintain a take-no-prisoners approach to all questions? Definitely not. Intellectual integrity implies—yes, even demands—that you be open to persuasion. You can change your mind for good reason and therefore agree with the crowd—if you are truly persuaded by new information, as distinguished from yielding to pressure to go along or conform with the group. In such a case, you show strength and exercise integrity by changing your position. Only when you act against your true position do you lose your integrity.

Trait #4: Be Consistent

Legacy achievers exhibit consistent behavior, and people who are consistent naturally become more influential. Think about the people who influence you the most. Do they haphazardly change stances on issues, or are they consistent in their beliefs?

Personally, I find it difficult to build relationships with inconsistent people. I never quite know where they stand on any given issue. I have difficulty trusting them.

Remember back to your days in high school. When a new semester began, you thought a laid-back, easy teacher was the greatest. But later in the semester when exam time came around, if that laid-back teacher poured on serious homework you may have felt betrayed by his or her inconsistency.

In contrast, you probably didn't like the tough teacher who dished out homework from the start, but eventually you came to expect the homework and just dealt with it. When exam time came, you were better prepared to study due to the teacher's consistent assignments.

In the end, you probably learned more from and respected the tough teacher. That teacher's influence over you far surpassed the other's.

Consistency is a building block for long-term relationships because security and consistency are interwoven. During a discussion on the benefits of consistency, a woman rejected this idea.

"If I'm consistent, I can't act spontaneously. And that's how I live my life," she said. "I'm spontaneous. That's who I am."

"Are you spontaneous all the time?" I asked.

"Yes."

"Well then," I said, "you're consistently spontaneous."

Although my response may have sounded flippant, her example illustrates a point about consistency. When you are around someone who always acts spontaneously, you know you have to be alert, stay on your toes, and be ready for quick changes. In her presence, you can find a certain security in knowing that something exciting could happen at any moment. Not everyone can appreciate this type of person, but if you can, such people are usually quite fun to have as friends.

TRAIT #5: MAINTAIN A HEALTHY OUTLOOK ON COMPETITION

Influential people have a tremendous understanding of their own competitive nature. We all inherently possess the desire to compete, even if only in some small way. Understandably, some people may want to reject the idea that everyone has a competitive nature, but that objection usually wanes when I explain that in my definition I include the desire to grow personally in knowledge and virtue. Either we desire to compete with ourselves or with others around us. Having the desire to compete does not always mean that we choose to compete. Knowing the right time, place, and reason to compete is essential to maintaining motivation.

The desire to compete is fueled both positively and negatively. Positive driving forces are things like enjoying a challenge or wanting to improve ourselves. Negative driving forces are related to envy, greed, jealousy, power, and runaway self-esteem.

Personal competition exists on two levels—internal and external. Internal competition is the contest between your current self and your past performances. This is often the desire to grow in knowledge and virtue. Internal competition propels people to outperform their own past in order to grow. External competition is competition with other people; for most of us, this means the people immediately around us.

Legacy achievers or integrity-based influencers control their competitive impulses better than most people. There are three types of competitive people: passive, addictive, and selective.

Passive Competitors

Some passive competitors deny having a competitive spirit, which really defies human nature. All people possess some sense of competition. Passively competitive people can accurately say they have great control over their competitive impulses, but to deny their existence is wrong.

Many passive competitors falsely claim they are not competitive because they don't want to put forth the necessary effort to achieve what they desire. Others claim to be noncompetitive because they fear failure.

Envy often drives these attitudes. Someone we'll call Bob claims he doesn't want a luxury car, yet he always knows who owns one in his circle of acquaintances. Bob makes a lot of sarcastic remarks about such people, saying things like, "They can't get attention any other way," and "No matter what wheels he has, he's still a fat chrome-dome."

It's a safe bet that Bob secretly lusts for a BMW of his own but knows he can't afford one. Instead of knuckling down to earn one or freeing himself of this envy by growing internally, he uses denial and attack as defense mechanisms.

On the other hand, legacy achievers who claim not to desire a luxury car have no interest in who drives what. At least two multibillionaires—the Reform Party's Ross Perot and Amazon.com's founder, Jeff Bezos—drive themselves around in modest cars. Do you think they know or care whether there's a Rolls Royce in every other garage on their street?

Truly passive competitors can become very influential because their integrity and low-key approach make them like the old E.F. Hutton slogan, "When they talk, people listen."

Addictive Competitors

The addictive competitor goes overboard on competition and has a difficult time controlling his or her desire to compete, even in trivial matters. Some addictive competitors seem to have a mechanism in their mind that connects the ability to win directly with their self-esteem. For this type of addictive competitor, the spirit of competition is not as important as winning. Other addictive competitors can't stand the idea of someone having something they don't, even if that something is simply the satisfaction of winning.

A great example of an addictive competitor is the guy who pulls up next to you at a red light and takes off like a drag racer when the light turns green. The addictive competitor must get in front of you even if he or she is not in a hurry. You'll often catch up with him a few blocks later to find him barely going the speed limit. The drag racer just had to be in the lead. He just *had to compete*—even if the other party was not even actively engaged in the contest.

Another example is the guy who gets angry over losing a card game with friends. He makes the others uncomfortable and loses their respect. An addictive competitor generally does not become an legacy achiever because he lacks influence. He also falls victim to object mentality. Instead of thinking of the other people in the game as people (subjects) who came to unwind before jumping back into a stressful week, he sees them as objects to be used for his own entertainment. They are to be defeated in order for him to feel good about himself.

Most people who get to know these people have a hard time taking them seriously; they treat everything as a competition and are always in high gear. They are often seen as one-dimensional, even if they are not. We have all run into this type of person at one time or another. Some of us, including myself, may occasionally act like this person to a lesser degree. But when you find yourself all wrapped up in a pointless competition yet having a hard time resolving it, you must view your actions as others do (pretty stupid), and get over it!

Selective Competitors

The selective competitor calculates when it is appropriate to compete. He or she carefully determines what drives their competitive spirit. Being a selective competitor makes a legacy achiever influential; the general public sees them as reasonable. Selective competitors are not only people who know when to compete, they also have an impressive winning record.

Selective competitors know when to compete and have an impressive winning record.

Selective competitors are winners because they take time to determine what is important to them and focus on developing the skills to accomplish it. This does not mean that they completely avoid things at which they do poorly. It simply means that they put those things in perspective when they participate in them.

For example, a selective competitor goes skiing with better skiers than herself, but she would not jump a cliff to prove that she is the best.

Selective competitors compete wisely. Unlike addictive competitors who try to force their way to victories, selective competitors use strategy and finesse to accomplish their ends.

An addictive competitor racing an Indy car finds it difficult to let other drivers pass him when stopping at the pit to fuel up and get a change of tires. The selective competitor sees the long-term value of the pit stop despite the temporary setback. This mentality keeps him in the race to its conclusion. Being a legacy achiever is all about a long-term perspective.

TRAIT #6: FOCUS ON CHARACTER

Your character is who you really are as a person while your reputation is merely what others think of you. Influential people feel good about how they present themselves to others, knowing they present the real person.

Sometimes simple advice is the most important advice. I can remember being told in my youth that if I always told the truth I'd never have to worry about remembering what I said. At the time I did not realize it, but I was being taught about integrity and character.

Legacy achievers wouldn't have it any other way. Projecting an image that is inconsistent with who you really are is very dangerous. Many politicians have become painfully aware of this. When politicians win an election on false pretenses, they run the risk of being found out. Not only is the potential embarrassment great for these people, but the lack of credibility that stems from such a practice can be devastating. When a man's character is under attack, he loses his influence.

Think of yourself as having a makeup similar to planet Earth. When you take a close look at yourself, you see a core, a mantel, and a surface—very much the same as our planet.

Your *core* is what you *really* believe as a person or who you really are. Your *mantle* is your past experiences in life (something we cannot change). And your *surface* is how you appear to others.

It is easy to assume that a person is the real deal because she looks good on the outside. But if you dig a little deeper, below the surface, you may find someone with core beliefs that don't match her surface. This swings both ways. Some people believe righteous things but are too weak to live in accordance with their belief. They become like Pontius Pilate, ruling against their better judgment because their actual beliefs are unpopular. On the other hand some people act righteous despite their ugly core. They do this only to manipulate others, as Robert Greene suggests.

We cannot change the past. Our mantle, or life experiences, may be filled with events that are not consistent with our current beliefs. It is more important that our core matches our surface than that our surface matches our mantle.

Because we all make mistakes, our integrity and character should not be measured only by what we have done in the past. More important, we should be measured by how well our *current* actions match our *current* core values and beliefs.

If you tried to measure integrity and character by past experiences alone you would have no hope of becoming a better person yourself. The catch here is that when you have behaved in a way that is inconsistent with your current core beliefs, it may take time for others to trust that you are truly different now. That is why legacy achievers pay close attention to make sure that how they act truly reflects who they are.

TRAIT #7: CULTIVATE COURAGE

Influential people are courageous. In chapter 2, I explained that being in balance is about participating in activities rather than just avoiding them. It takes courage to face many of the challenges we encounter each day. It also takes courage to admit our mistakes to ourselves and to others.

The opposite of courage is fear. Some people argue that fear provides a valuable service in preserving life by causing us to avoid danger. However, a closer look at fear reveals that other emotions and actions preserve us from danger. Fear simply provides an alarm. When faced with danger, fear is an immediate response, but it paralyzes you if you don't convert your fear into a positive act. Therefore, fear triggers other responses, such as courage, to guide us to safety.

Courage consists of two parts. The first part is focus. The more you focus on what you must do, the less you will be inhibited by weakening emotions such as fear.

When a wide receiver focuses clearly on the ball being thrown to him, he increases his chances of catching it. On the other hand, if he fears being tackled or fears dropping the ball, his focus is distracted and he reduces his odds for success tremendously. Focusing on the job at hand keeps

MOTIVATION = Balance + **Influence** + (Creativity + Humor) − Runaway Self-Esteem negative emotions at bay. But to eliminate them we must add the second part of courage—enthusiasm.

If the football player is focused but not enthusiastic, he leaves room for fear to creep in. Enthusiasm energizes focus and allows you to get the results you desire.

Legacy achievers, who plan for the future, often do not recognize themselves as being courageous. When you prepare for a challenge you are about to face, you enter the situation with focus and enthusiasm. When that combination becomes a habit, you'll become more influential because your example will precede your words.

A champion high diver who prepares for a difficult dive does not think about courage when taking the platform. Rather, the diver thinks about being prepared, having practiced their technique; neither fear nor courage register at this time. On this high performance level, the mind simply focuses enthusiastically on the task at hand.

If everyone is thinking alike then someone isn't thinking.

—George S. Patton, Jr.

Creativity and Humor

Creativity, an important tactical tool for developing motivation, has a rare quality. The more you use it, the more you have at your command. Creativity is far more than a renewable resource; it's a fast-breeding reactor churning out more of itself every time it's turned on. So turn it on more often.

Legacy achievers show us that motivation is triggered during challenging times when we try to think of a solution to our problems. Unmotivated people often feel there are no solutions for the challenges they face. This feeling stems from a hope-destroying lack of creativity. The simple act of deciding to use creativity to cope with our immediate situation will give us hope, and hope will motivate us to find the workable solutions we need.

If you trap ourselves into feeling there's no way out of a problem, you shut down. You think, "There's no reason to try. There's just no solution; why bother?"

Occasionally, in the midst of what appears to be a hopeless situation, you hear a story about an amazing person who rose above a similar situation, and you take heart. That person's solution renews your motivation.

Creative thinking creates unique solutions.

Tapping into your own creativity helps you maneuver around obstacles that block your motivation. Creative thinking creates unique solutions. In order to increase your creative skills, we must first recognize five common stumbling blocks to creativity.

Five Stumbling Blocks to Creativity

While all of us have some capacity for creativity, a number of things can interfere with your ability to think and act in creative ways. Here are the five worst obstacles, and how you can overcome them.

    1. "Somebody has already thought of it."
When you rest on your laurels or sit on your creativity, believing you've already thought of every possible approach to a problem with no solution in sight, it's only a matter of time before you're proven wrong. At such times you say, "Why didn't I think of that?" or worse, "Why did I think of that and not act on it?"

Consider an idea for a new product. Have you ever thought of a product that would solve an everyday consumer problem but say to yourself, "Ah, someone probably has invented it by now"? Then two years later you read an article about America's latest millionaire, only to find out that her ticket to fame and fortune was your idea. After trying to figure out how she "stole your idea," logic asserts itself and you realize that she had the same idea but was wise enough to bring it to fruition. The solution is simple. Begin each problem-solving session with the attitude that something new is out there. Know that you will find a solution given enough time to come up with one. This attitude of victory just around the corner will motivate you to come up with answers. The opposite attitude, awaiting certain defeat, will always lead to destruction.

2. "It's good enough."

An "It's good enough" attitude stifles creativity and stops motivation. A one-sided sliding-door minivan is a fine illustration of *good enough* thinking. Back in the 1980s, this new adaptation of the older, larger vans was a very creative idea. However, this new family vehicle, designed for convenience, had one of the most inconvenient features available—a rear sliding door on only one side of the car.

Obviously the world loved the idea of a minivan because many were sold. But when the concept was developed further and two-sliding-door vans became available, sales of the improved models skyrocketed.

The car manufacturers who had an *it's-good-enough* attitude were caught behind the eight ball. Before they could redesign and retool their vehicles, their competitors had skimmed off the cream of demand for the new double-door minivan.

3. "I'm not creative. I'm more analytical."
If we lock our minds into thinking, "I'm not creative; I'm analytical," we must reconsider our argument. Analysis requires creativity. Creativity is the process that allows us to analyze effectively. So if one is analytical, one is also creative.

Unfortunately, many people take themselves out of the creativity game before the buzzer sounds. I can assure you, we are all creative in various ways. Like a muscle, the more we exercise our creativity, the stronger it gets.

4. "What if I make a fool of myself?"
Creativity requires some level of risk, and we often fear taking risks. The fear of failure

is a top creativity roadblock. We sometimes ask ourselves, "But what if I make a fool of myself?" or, "What if I make a mistake?" If everyone had that attitude there would literally have been no inventions since the beginning of time. If Edison would have stopped at 9,999 broken bulbs or the Wright Brother after dozens of flightless attempts, we would still be in the dark and on the ground today.

Nearly everything that is invented must fail before it works. So if your attitude is "What if I fail?" you're asking the wrong question. The question is "What happens when I fail?" The answer is simple: Press on until it is no longer relevant or until you get it right.

One of the unfortunate misperceptions about success is similar to the misconception I addressed early in the book regarding motivation. The misconception is that motivated people are motivated naturally; the truth is that motivated people struggle with their own motivation, just like unmotivated people do. The difference is that motivated people press on by using the strategies outlined in this book.

It's the same when it comes to success. Most people hear musicians in their glory on CD or watch an actor brilliantly bring a character to life on the big screen. They never see the mistakes and failures that took place before the production was ready for consumption. Creativity is the same way. Mistakes are not only for the people who fail. They are for anyone who tries in the first place. Begin with that mindset, and you'll get past the fear of failure or looking silly.

5. "I don't have time for this."
Creative thinking can be time consuming. Tapping into your creativity can be an exercise in patience; solutions to most problems usually don't readily appear. Often, you must contemplate, process, and reprocess information to find imaginative answers to your questions and concerns. Like Edison, we must contemplate, process, and repeat our efforts—until the light goes on.

WE ALL POSSESS CREATIVITY

Some people spend little time on original thinking, fully convinced of their lack of creativity. These people can be quite convincing when defending their lack of creative skills. But ironically, creativity is the only explanation for their clever and powerful arguments, which defeats their point.

We all possess creativity. Children play creatively throughout the day as their attention wanders from toy to toy. Even without toys, kids find creative ways to play.

While all my children are creative, my daughter, Nicole, provides our family with the most visual examples of her creativity. When she was only five, she colored, decorated, and redesigned anything she could get her hands on.

Unfortunately, sometimes her younger brother, Ethan, was the only malleable object she could find. She dressed him up outrageously, cracking up the entire family. Since he was too young to understand what she was doing to him, I used to rescue him out of good conscience. But sometimes we seized the opportunity to take a few pictures first, in order to make his sixteenth birthday a lot of fun.

But as we rush into adulthood, we are often stripped of our creative confidence. In Daniel Burrus's book *Technotrends* (Harper Business), he references studies showing children losing as much as 90 percent of their creative expression between the ages of five and seven. At around five, children enter formal educational systems and must conform to a more standardized way of thinking.

Conformity can suppress our creativity. Although I'm a big believer in the benefits of conformity to enhance order in society, certain forms of conformity can flatten originality. When we lose the ability to think creatively, we all suffer. As a result, there are fewer new light bulbs to make our future a brighter place.

When we lose the ability to think creatively, we all suffer.

An excellent way to unlock creativity is to allow your mind to brainstorm combinations of two previously separate concepts—such as lightning and power, or two sliding doors and a minivan. You may find this exercise surprisingly rewarding and often very amusing.

We all posses the power to be creative, as psychologists

who study creativity all agree. I urge you to tap into your own creative capabilities.

Humor

A sense of humor is the component in the Formula for Motivation that can be a breath of fresh air when we need it most, reinvigorating ourselves and our motivation. Humor has three important benefits that help legacy achievers increase and maintain motivation. They are:

~ Better health
~ Greater acceptance of mistakes—our own and others'
~ Increased ability to influence others

BETTER HEALTH

Lee Berk, PhD, MPH, and Stanley Tan, an endocrinologist at California's Loma Linda University Medical Center, have been studying the effects of laughter on health. Since stress weakens the immune system, these doctors set out to determine whether and to what extent laughter strengthens the immune system.

Berk and Tan took blood samples from subjects in ten-minute intervals before, during, and after the subjects watched videos of comedians. Humor was found to trigger physiological processes similar to exercise. The group of people who watched the comedians showed an increase in good hormones (endorphins and neurotransmitters) as well as two other hormones known to decrease levels of stress (cortisol and adrenaline). Laughter increases the number of cells that produce antibodies, such as T-cells, which combat viruses.

Their research delivered a clear message: laughing more means you're less likely to end up in a sickbed, and if you do get sick, you'll be back on your feet sooner. Now that's motivating!

On average, children laugh 150 times per day. Adults on the other hand, laugh only ten times a day. When adults watch children play we often say, "Where do they get all that energy?" I believe children's ready laughter is the source of much of their energy. How much more energy would we adults have if we laughed as much as children?

GREATER ACCEPTANCE OF MISTAKES— OUR OWN AND OTHERS'

Human's aptness to increase our capacity to understand and forgive mistakes can be illustrated through common occurrences. All of us at one time or another are frustrated by people whom we claim "just don't get it" (whatever "it" may be in that circumstance).

For example, take people who drive slowly in the fast lane. Have you ever noticed them doing this with a car next to them so you can't pass? This drives most people crazy. When it happens to you, frustration turns to anger and anger turns to irrational assertions. You think, "They're trying to ruin my day! That idiot must have gotten on the phone last night and called a few slow-driving friends just to tick me off!"

Now totally irrationally, you imagine the conversation, "Hey, Joe. What are you doing at seven o'clock tomorrow morning? See, I really want to bug this guy in a blue

MOTIVATION = Balance + Influence + (Creativity + Humor) – Runaway Self-Esteem sedan. I'll get in front of his car, and you box him in on the left, that way he can't pass. He'll go crazy. While we're at it, do you know anyone who's good at tailgating?"

Still boxed in, you conjure up countless new laws to stop stupid driving. "Fine them a thousand dollars for each minute I'm late for work. No. Put people like that in jail for life. No. Put people like that in solitary confinement so they don't make the other inmates late, too. No one should have to suffer like this!"

Finally, the slow driver hogging the fast lane moves to the slow lane, allowing you to pass. You can't wait to get a good look at the guy. You creep up next to him only to find that he just wasn't paying attention. He *just didn't get it*. He wasn't aware of your existence, let alone your anger. You say to yourself, "What a fool!"

Then one day you find yourself daydreaming in the fast lane. "Oops! I sure hope no one's behind me." But, of course, someone in a hurry is tailgating you. Embarrassed, you move to the slow lane, pretending to adjust your radio so when the guy passes he won't think *you just didn't get it*!

It's a good time to laugh at yourself.

When you laugh at yourself, you learn to accept other people's mistakes with greater understanding. Laughing at your own mistakes is sometimes your only choice, outside of crying.

Years ago, as a guest on a Chicago radio show, I told the host I was searching for stories about people who *just don't get it*. The phone lines lit up. Furious people vented about others who *just didn't get it*. Some callers complained about people who stand in line at fast-food places for a long time, then when they finally reach the counter, they can't decide what to order. Others complained about people who stand still at the top of an escalator when they reach the top so other passengers have no place to exit. You name it, they complained about it!

One story came from a man who asked his girlfriend to buy a newspaper from a corner vending machine. He gave her fifty cents and away she went, but she soon returned empty-handed.

"Where's my paper?"

"The machine was empty."

"Where's my fifty cents?"

"I don't have it anymore."

"Why not?"

"I didn't know the machine was empty until I dropped the quarters in the slot and opened the door because the newspaper in the window was in the way."

Now put yourself in his place. If your reaction to her oversight is frustration, then you rob yourself of a chance for laughter and create irritation, which steals your energy. If you really think about it, chances are you'll remember one or two "vending machine experiences" of your own.

I ran across a silly story in a book entitled *The Best Book of Lists Ever*. While warming up for the New York Golden Gloves Championship in 1992, a boxer named Daniel Caruso punched himself so hard he couldn't compete.

You may think to yourself, "How stupid could you be? Punch yourself?" But if you're name is Dave Durand, you'd say, "Funny, but I can relate."

In my own kitchen one time, I showed a friend the

difference between tai fighting and kickboxing. In a simple demonstration of how tai fighters strike with their elbows, I accidentally punched myself in the nose and broke it. Whack! Crack!

There I stood with an amazed look on my face. My look of disbelief was only outdone by my friend's shocked expression.

I pushed my nose back in place right then and there. "Is it straight?" I asked, like I was fixing my tie.

"No," my friend said. "A little to the right. There you go."

Oh yes, I felt pain, but I laughed at my odd situation. I never met Caruso, the boxer, but I sure can relate to his story.

Here's the problem. Laughing at yourself means humbling yourself, and that won't work if you're filled with pride. The problem is that pride is blinding. So here's what you do. Begin with the understanding that *everyone* is prideful. Your pride may be manifested differently based on the temperament you have, but it's still present.

If you begin by asking yourself how you can reduce your pride, instead of whether or not you have pride, you'll be more apt to overcome it. The result will increase your ability to laugh at yourself and at the other oddities in life that are worth a chuckle.

INCREASED ABILITY TO INFLUENCE OTHERS

Chapter 3 discussed how being influential has a motivating effect on your life. A good sense of humor can be an effective and inspiring part of influence. When you make people laugh, at yourself or at other things, you make them feel good. People pay psychiatrists thousands of dollars to help them feel better, but one good laugh can do a person more good than six months of therapy—and it won't cost a dime.

We all have a tendency to like people who make us laugh, and people we like have the greatest edge when it comes to influencing us.

Creativity and Humor Form a Dynamic Duo

Creativity plays a big role in our sense of humor. Laughter generates creativity. Creativity creates laughter. It's not everybody's aim in life to be a comedian, but we can all learn from a comedian's creative perspective.

Comedians can take a normal life situation and, through creativity, twist it into a crazy scenario. The resulting laughter motivates the comedian to be even more creative. In turn, you enjoy more humor.

When comedian and talk show host Johnny Carson ended his last *Tonight Show*, people cried. When Seinfeld closed his series, fans across the country suffered from what they called "Seinfeld withdrawal." Why? Because we lost our connection with people who made us laugh daily.

Laughter is one of the greatest gifts you can give someone.

Laughter is one of the greatest gifts you can give someone. We often feel grateful to people who make us laugh. In turn, we should spread a little laughter ourselves. All of us, from the class clown to the most serious and studious person, have some positive quality that can evoke laughter and joy in others.

Life is just too strange not to find the humor in it. Engage your sense of humor. Connect your creativity and your funny bone. After all, laughter helps us move past pain, freeing and inspiring the creativity from which motivation springs.

Conclusion

 Applying the Formula for Motivation enhances life tremendously. The lessons we have learned from legacy achievers demonstrate that clearly. I will summarize the key points in the Formula for Motivation (balance + influence + creativity and humor—runaway self-esteem) and then conclude with two stories I hope will add to your perspective on motivation.

The Pursuit of Life's Perfect Balance

Balancing your life by spinning the six plates of life—family, financial responsibility, health, social contributions, education and vocation, and faith—is essential. Each balance point has the power to enhance your drive and appreciation for life; each of them also has the power to destroy your perseverance. Having a daily focus on each of the six balance points is the main strategic key to unlocking perpetual motivation.

You need to be focused on a perfect target. You will never reach perfection, but using it as a target brings clarity to your goals. If we simply focus on doing our best, how will we know if we have arrived? How will we know if we couldn't continue to improve? The answer is difficult because being our best is hard to define. So stay focused on the limitless target of perfection, but like a pilot and copilot, accept the times when you're a little off course as part of your journey toward life's perfect balance.

Integrity-Based Influence

We need to communicate with others to find and maintain balance in our lives and to become motivated by what we stand for. If we simply rely on the techniques taught by today's pop culture trainers, we will only be effective for the short run.

The damage done to our reputation as well as our conscience by acting without integrity can be difficult—or almost impossible—to repair. Because of this we must use integrity-based influence. That is, we must keep the good of the party we are influencing in mind. We must develop the seven integrity-based influencing characteristics of legacy achievers:

1. Keep your emotions on a leash
2. Use harmony and conviction in verbal communication

3. Anticipate communication challenges and opportunities

4. Be consistent

5. Maintain a healthy outlook on competition

6. Focus on character

7. Cultivate courage

Creativity and Humor

Developing our creativity keeps us open to life's opportunities. We may feel trapped in life if we can't think of viable solutions to the problems we face. Our unique creativity is the answer to such problems.

Our sense of humor can be essential in staying healthy, accepting ourselves and other people, and moving past difficult times. When we find humor in life, we can put our worries aside long enough to develop creative solutions. The result leads to our perpetual motivation.

Runaway Self-Esteem

Possibly the most mind-bending insight acquired by reading this book will be a new perspective on self-esteem. *Having* a high self-esteem is not a problem. Problems with self-esteem arise from how we attain it and how much we focus on it.

A high self-esteem should be the result of positive actions that re measured by external standards, as well as our own. If we rely only on our personal standards—as many authors and psychiatrists recommend—we will be confused and overwhelmed by the ambiguity this brings.

Likewise, if we try to build a false self-esteem through positive affirmations, which really constitute nothing more than lying to ourselves, we will never truly attain it.

We must submit to standards set by the people and systems we respect, such as our family, corporation, or church. This will provide practical reasons for feeling good about ourselves and our accomplishments.

Let me emphasize the most important point in the chapter on runaway self-esteem: If we focus on serving others before serving ourselves, we will become happy with who we are. We will be motivated to continue striving for the important things in life.

A Double Dose of Motivation

The following stories have morals that will broaden our perspective on the value of achieving and maintaining motivation to live a good life. They will help you as you begin living a life filled with perpetual motivation.

If we live by the principles that legacy achievers have taught us by their example, we are bound to find happiness. Unfortunately this thought may give us the urge to look forward to the future and forget to enjoy today. Not to worry. When you think about it, we never actually live in the future. We only live in the present.

JOHN'S STORY

Johnny was anxious to be big. He knew life would be better when he could see over the countertops. When the great day arrived and he realized his goal, he knew he was almost old enough to go to kindergarten, where the fun would begin.

After the first week of kindergarten, Johnny could not stop thinking about what the first graders where doing in their classroom. He couldn't wait until he was in a real grade. After he arrived in first grade, he repeated the same pattern of fantasizing about the following year. He did this year after year. By the time Johnny was in eighth grade, he knew he was only one year away from the ultimate life experience, high school. He wished each day away until high school finally arrived.

Johnny saw the upperclassmen and knew that they had it made. His desire to be a king at school as a senior was great. That's when life would really begin. During Johnny's senior year, he began to look into colleges. The thought of complete independence captured his attention. Every day of his senior year was spent longing for the freedom of college.

When John finally went off to university, he began learning about science. He couldn't wait to some day be the head of a research company. He studied hard so he could finish his education as fast as possible. He graduated with honors and found a job.

He hated being at the bottom of the ladder. His boss seemed to have it made. Jonathon couldn't wait to have people reporting to him. In a few years he was promoted. He knew he was close to having it all. He just needed to buy the new car he had his eye on. Then he would have it made.

He bought the car but felt something was missing. He thought, "If I can climb the ladder at work, I will be able to buy a house." Owning a home would be the answer to what was missing. So Jonathon worked hard and received a promotion. He was able to buy a house. But the house felt empty. Jonathon realized that his happiness would finally arrive when he was married.

Being attractive and having a dynamic personality made it easy for Jonathon to meet people. After a brief time dating, Jonathon met Miss Right and they married. But he thought there had to more. Having children would be the most fulfilling thing life could offer. So they had two children. But the work of taking care of infants and toddlers was more than Jonathon expected.

When his children were out of diapers and able to talk, being a dad would finally be fulfilling, he knew. When his kids were able to walk and talk, Jonathon realized they were only a few years away from being able to play catch. He knew it would be the time when they would bond. As the children grew and Jonathon turned into a taxi driver for them and their friends, he became eager for the day when his kids could drive. When the kids were older and acted as teenagers act, Jonathon exclaimed to himself that he could see the light at the end of the tunnel when the kids would go off to college and he would have the house back the way it was before he had children.

That's when it hit him.

For the first time, Jonathon realized that he wanted something he had already had. He had never stopped to enjoy today; the realization hit him hard. What he was experiencing today was what he had looked forward to yesterday. Failing to understand this reality had kept him from living his life. With more than half of his life over, Jonathon had just started to live. It was time for him to meet the people in his life today, to live his life today, and to forget about hankering after tomorrow until it becomes today.

Each day is filled with treasures we need to discover and enjoy. Challenges sometimes make those treasures hard to find, but when we put our faith in God and focus on the people around us rather than on ourselves we can find fulfillment in our difficulties.

With more than half of his life over, Jonathon had just started to live.

Hopefully you are able to gather some insight from the formula for living a motivated life and from the legacy achievers who practice these principles. It is interesting to note that most legacy achievers would not categorize themselves as such. In a recent conversation I had with a legacy achiever who read this book, he said, "Wow, I felt like you were writing about me when you wrote about people falling short of being legacy achievers."

I was surprised by his comment. I know him well, and he has all the traits and habits of a legacy achiever. He is a dedicated father and husband with clear priorities, placing his family ahead of his job. He has reached business objectives and goals most people only dream about. He is responsible with his finances. He is a spiritual man focused on an increased faith, and he maintains great health. He is always motivated and is a very happy person. That's the point. Although he does not see himself as a legacy achiever, he is one. He is in a continual growth mode and finds happiness in the process. He is excited about continuing to learn and develop and is comfortable with his commitment to this lifelong journey. However, because he is focused on bettering himself, he feels he is not yet a legacy achiever.

We can always improve, no matter who we are. If we stop growing, we will die emotionally and physically. At the same time, we need to find happiness in the journey. If we wait for ourselves to arrive at a state of perfection while we are on earth in order to attain happiness, we will never find it.

THE LONG DAY

The morning was so crisp it felt surreal. I knew it was going to be a great day. Although my travels have taken me to many places, I had never witnessed the scenic beauty I took in that day in the Rocky Mountains of British Columbia. I had arrived from Vancouver, after dark, the evening before in a rented Ford Explorer. Now the beauty of the landscape lay before me.

I would be finished with my meeting fairly early and could then enjoy the breathtaking view on the seven-hour drive back to Vancouver, this time in daylight. From there I would cruise the Pacific Coast by ferryboat for an hour before arriving on Vancouver Island and settling into my hotel, where I expected to enjoy a tasty meal and catch up on some reading. I would then get to sleep at a reasonable hour. At least that was my plan.

By late morning I was on my way, knowing I would be seeing one of the world's most incredible landscapes. The drive leaving Kelowna was filled with eye candy almost beyond visual taste bud capacity.

The jagged mountains in the distance melted into the

closer rolling mountains that sloped into Lake Okanagan. The lake is famous for Ogopogo, as its version of the Loch Ness monster is called. This sixty-mile-long, nine hundred-foot deep body of water draws the mind beyond its idyllic beauty into the mystery of the legend. Even people who consider themselves too sophisticated to believe in a lake monster glance at the water in hopes of catching a glimpse of what they claim not to believe in.

As I drove out of the city and entered the heights of the massive Canadian Rockies, the world changed. My radio did not come in and my cell phone was out of range. I was alone in the midst of the beauty of God's creation, overwhelmed by the views surrounding me.

The seasons seemed to change from summer to spring as I went higher and higher. A snowstorm at the peak of the drive made it feel like winter. I couldn't wait to complete my trip to Vancouver Island, which is known for having some of the most beautiful gardens in the world. I was right; today was a great day.

Making good time, I entered the city of Vancouver as planned, six hours after starting. Unfortunately, the rush hour had just begun.

Vancouver's beauty is as impressive as its road system is not. Many travelers get to enjoy the landscape from their car windows longer than they would prefer. I was about to enjoy the view from my car for an hour longer than I had planned. Mentally I could handle it—until I made a huge mistake.

To save time I decided to rely on directional signs to get me to the ferry instead of stopping for directions. This soon put me in the middle of downtown Vancouver stuck in a lane of traffic that, before I could get out of, forced me onto the Lion Gate Bridge. A sign seemed to say it was the right way to go.

Wrong.

My penalty was an hour and a half ride across a bridge spanning less than a half mile, plus an additional hour and half to get back. All of a sudden my seven-hour car ride had turned into at least ten, probably eleven, hours. Now time pressed on me. I asked for directions, and things seemed like they were about to get better.

Wrong again.

My friendly direction givers spoke with conviction when they told me how to find the ferry, only ten minutes away. But somehow I was misled. I traveled everywhere a ten-minute drive would cover. No ferry.

My blood felt searing hot under my skin. My anger clouded my mind so much I was driving recklessly. I even ran a red light because I wasn't paying attention, avoiding a side-on collision by about a half second. I hate to imagine how the lives of all those involved in the near accident would have changed had either car been moving at a slightly different speed.

I had trouble calming down. When I did, I went to a gas station where two young gentlemen looked like they might be able to help me. I will never forget telling them to talk to me like I was two bricks short of a load.

"Guys, keep the directions simple because I must be lacking the mental capacity to follow basic instructions today. Everyone tells me the ferry is ten minutes away, and I have been everywhere within ten minutes from here.

Speak slowly and draw me pictures because I am at my wits' end!"

They laughed and said, "Ten minutes, no way. The ferry is at least an hour from here."

I couldn't believe it—a whole hour away! At this point I had forgotten about getting to the hotel in time for a nice dinner; I just wanted to get to the ferry before it sailed at 11:00 P.M. I had to catch the last boat to the island or miss my meeting the following morning. It was already after ten o'clock so I had to move fast.

Because I was irrationally suspicious of everyone's ability to provide sound directions, I crossed the street to see if I could get corroboration. To my delight I received confirming directions. Out of curiosity I asked, "How long will it take to get there?"

"About ten minutes."

I almost fell over. How could that be? I didn't waste time worrying about it and arrived barely soon enough to drive aboard the night's last boat. I parked my car on the ferry's lower parking level along with what looked like several hundred other cars.

Feeling nauseous from hunger, headache, and bad attitude, I struggled to climb to the cafeteria-style restaurant on the ferry's top floor—four decks up if I remember correctly. I wanted to eat something and then rest until we reached the island.

At the counter I selected my food and went to a quiet corner to relax. Right away a hairy lumberjack-looking fellow, who apparently needed to talk to someone, sat down next to me. I was not in the mood for conversation.

"So where are you headed?"

I thought his question was a bit silly since the ferry had only one destination—the island—but something about him made me want to be polite. "Victoria."

"Where in Victoria?"

"I don't know yet. I'll choose a hotel when I get there."

What he said next ended my coma-like state and put me into a close cousin of the fight or flight mode, weakness forgotten.

"You're screwed. The whole island is sold out because of the jazz festival."

I jumped up, ran four flights down to my car, got my cell phone, returned to a tourist brochure display on the top floor, and started calling hotels. Finally I found what I'm sure was the last hotel room on the entire island.

I soon found out why it had earned the distinction of still being available. The two-story hotel was smaller and dirtier than a university frat house. It was after 1 A.M. when I got there, stumbling with exhaustion and not too clearheaded. After checking for roaches and rats, I tried to call my wife.

I always call Lisa when I arrive at a hotel, no matter how late. She always wants to know where I am and how I'm doing; I also want to know how she and the kids are doing. I couldn't get through on my cell phone, and my calling card didn't work. I would have to talk to her the next day.

I slept like a rock. The next morning, feeling refreshed and eager to start the new day, I decided to say a kind word to the hotel owner before going on my way. As I walked down, I met him.

He looked at me with great concern and said, "I'm so sorry." I glanced over my shoulder to see who he was talking to, but saw no one.

"I'm so sorry," he said again.

"About what?"

He looked puzzled and then added a so: "I'm so, so sorry."

"About what?" I repeated, louder this time.

"The fire," he said, looking amazed.

"The fire? What fire?"

In the middle of the night the hotel had caught on fire and was evacuated, he told me. The street had been lined with fire engines and teeth-chattering hotel guests in pajamas.

I had slept through the whole thing, and no one knew I was in the hotel while it was burning. My wife didn't know where I was; no one knew.

Then it hit me: I was being watched over and cared for. During the previous mistake- and blunder-filled day, I had never stopped to appreciate my greatest possession, the gift of life. Even narrowly escaping death while running the red light did not get me to appreciate life the way I did that morning.

Then it hit me: I was being watched over and cared for.

My attitude became one of gratitude. It had been eight years since I began studying motivation and life balance, but it took only one twenty-four-hour period to convince me that a simple appreciation for my gift of life is a powerful motivation for living the best life I am capable of living.

Although not a formal part of the Formula for Motivation, the concept of appreciating life resides in the hearts of legacy achievers. Take an inventory of what God has given you. When we have a true appreciation for life, it will be reflected by our love for others, our peace during challenging times, and our ability to stay motivated.

Along the road, there will be challenges. Here's a helpful thought to carry with you: everyone is great at being great when things are going great, but truly great people are great at being great when things aren't going so great. When faced with challenges, look at the ways your life will improve when you gain the experience and skills it will take to overcome them.

We don't need to become famous, rich, or popular to become a legacy achiever. All we need to do is to stay loyal to the things that are most important in life. Through this focus, we will find motivation and make an impact that will be remembered as our legacy.

God bless!

To invite Dave to speak at your next company or organization event please contact him at:

dave@davedurand.com
and visit:
www.davedurand.com

To order other inspiring Dave Durand products including his patented time management planner, the Balander™ visit:

www.balander.com

NOTES

NOTES

NOTES

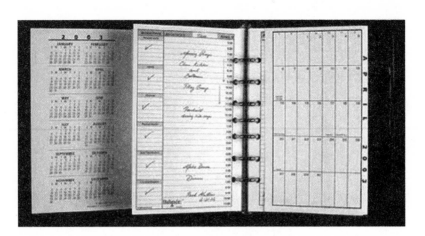

About The Author

The Crossroad Publishing Company is honored to welcome Dave Durand to our list. Many business people are already familiar with Dave's work from his corporate seminars and lectures. Others have come to know him from his Relevant Radio weekly program and his earlier books and programs, including the Balander program that he describes in this book. However you meet Dave, you'll enjoy his boundless energy and his genuine interest in helping others achieve their dreams.

The science of motivation is often seen as an issue for business people and consultants. When you watch Dave on DVD and read his books, you'll begin to look at motivation in a new light, as something that affects all of us in our daily lives. These days, all of us have to become our own managers, and Dave gives us the tools for doing this in an effective, and morally centered, way.

We have benefited from Dave's insights in our own work and lives, and we think you will, too.